Organic
KITCHEN
Gardening

Organic
KITCHEN
Gardening

A guide to growing produce in small urban areas

BARBARA SEGALL

New Holland

First published in 2002 by
New Holland Publishers (UK) Ltd
London · Cape Town · Sydney · Auckland

Garfield House
86–88 Edgware Road
London W2 2EA
United Kingdom
www.newhollandpublishers.com

80 McKenzie Street
Cape Town 8001
South Africa

Level 1, Unit 4, 14 Aquatic Drive
Frenchs Forest, NSW 2086
Australia

218 Lake Road
Northcote, Auckland
New Zealand

ISBN 1 84330 326 4

Editor: Gillian Haslam
Designer: Lisa Tai
Picture researcher: Joanne Beardwell
Illustrations: Kate Simunek

Editorial Direction: Rosemary Wilkinson
Project Editor: Clare Johnson
Production: Hazel Kirkman

10 9 8 7 6 5 4 3 2 1

Reproduction by Modern Age Repro, Hong Kong
Printed and bound by Times Offset (M) SDN BHD,
Malaysia

half title page: Nasturtium flowers and yellow courgette fruits combine well in a deep, wide, elegant wooden container made for a patio or a rooftop garden.

title page: Every space, no matter how small, such as this curved bed, holding lettuces and herbs, offers planting opportunities for the dedicated small-space gardener.

above: Attractively coloured and with interesting foliage texture, lettuces 'Tom Thumb', 'Lollo Rosso' and 'Lollo Biondo' thrive early in the season in the protective environment of a stylish glass cloche.

CONTENTS

WITHDRAWN

Introduction 6

CHAPTER 1 Getting Started 10

CHAPTER 2 Garden Layouts 30

CHAPTER 3 Growing in Containers 42

CHAPTER 4 Growing Vegetables 52

CHAPTER 5 Fruit 68

CHAPTER 6 Garden Plans 82

Further Reading 94

Useful Addresses 94

Index 96

INTRODUCTION

Food miles – the distance that foodstuffs travel on their way from their place of origin to a supermarket near you – are part of everyday parlance and although the journey is now amazingly quick compared with what it used to be, it still takes days off the freshness of the food. It is a simple fact that by growing fruit and vegetables yourself, you can enjoy them after the shortest possible trip between harvest basket and plate. Because you are the harvester, you can pick the fruit and vegetables at their peak, rather than a few days past their best.

As you are the gardener, you can decide the amount of chemical intervention used to control the inevitable pests and diseases that will vie with you to devour your produce. Whether you are 100 per cent organic or choose to use a little pesticide, at least you will know how the plants have been grown.

I first started growing vegetables when I lived in a flat in London. I had a small allotment so soon mastered the art of growing quantity in a limited space. Although I now have a large country garden, I still grow my vegetables in small rectangular raised beds, within flower borders and amongst herbs and edible flowers. I have particular vegetable favourites and grow tomatoes, pumpkins and courgettes (which demand larger spaces), beans and year-round salad leaves as my main crops each year.

In this book I have selected some of the varieties that have given the best results for my small

△ Here a balcony wall provides shelter for low-growing or mound-forming herbs such as creeping thyme, sage, chives, parsley and borage. They are growing in a specially constructed, deep planter, running along the outer edge of the balcony. The herbs are combined with ornamental plants such as the silver-leaved senecio.

spaces and provided the basic information you need for your first foray into urban kitchen gardening. The book covers the techniques for preparing the soil, producing the plants and outlines the small spaces that you are likely to encounter. It also provides practical suggestions for making those sites both productive and ornamental, and offers some design suggestions for particular situations.

Growing your own vegetables is one of gardening's great pleasures. Kitchen gardens have evolved from purely practical production areas attached to large houses into ornamental yet productive gardens for everyone. Ornament comes in foliage colour, shape and texture, in flowers and fruit, and in the combination of crops and garden designs. Picking fresh crops through the year provides high nutrition, taste-packed rewards unmatched by supermarket produce.

SUCCESS ON A SMALL SCALE

Small-space vegetable growers are skilled in the art of filling every bit of the garden with productive plants. In addition, they have perfected the art of using vegetables and herbs rather than flowers to beautify their small vegetable areas. In a large garden the vegetable patch – seen by some as more functional than attractive – is often kept out of sight, separated from the flower garden. In the small garden where space is at a premium, this segregation is an out-of-place luxury.

Even in the smallest city garden, there is sufficient space and opportunity for the determined fruit and vegetable grower to plant a wide range of produce. Windowboxes, containers of all shapes and sizes, hanging baskets and growbags are among the challenging sites for the urban kitchen gardener. The small-space vegetable grower has to adopt one or two strategies to ensure a regular supply of vegetables that suit the site and their own appetite. Fresh produce,

straight from the garden to the plate is the prize, and in a small garden it is won with a combination of work and ingenuity.

Planning and making the choices that suit your tastebuds and garden spaces are the keys to success in the small city vegetable garden. Plants may have to work hard for their place, providing

▽ Lettuces keep close company with cauliflowers during the early stages of growing. By the time the cauliflowers mature and fill out, the lettuces will have been harvested.

good flavour, ornament and nutrition. Effectively they become double duty plants, providing a double function of ornament and use. For example, instead of growing an apple tree which will take up a fair amount of space, plant a row of low-growing apples trained into cordons to form a step-over hedge (see page 70). This will provide attractive flowers in spring, abundant delicious and attractive-looking fruit in autumn and will make a useful boundary for part of the garden.

CHOOSING CROPS

Small-space gardening has several advantages over large scale gardening, and with clever planning you can keep a succession of fresh, home-grown produce ready for harvest through the year. But you do have to make choices. You have to decide what you will grow, how and more importantly where you will grow it. Then you have to manage the sowing and growing so you have a regular supply of seasonal food throughout the year.

The first rule is to plant what you enjoy most. Fresh leaves for salad mixes, edible flowers and various coloured lettuces may be your summertime choice, while for winter you may decide that you cannot live without a daily pick of spicy oriental salad leaves. Of course, if there is a particular vegetable or fruit that you would eat on a regular basis, glut or no glut, then plant that in profusion and make the most of it.

Bulk produce and large, thuggish plants such as cabbages which take up a great deal of space will not be options for the small-space vegetable gardener. In small spaces growing large quantities of anything will not be possible, and in any case, that would defeat the object of the fresh fast food you are harvesting.

Vegetable growing is seeing a resurgence in popularity and seed companies around the world are promoting a wide range of vegetables. Many of them offer small vegetable plants for sale, relieving the small-space grower of the early part of the crop production. The choice of vegetables and fruit and especially of old, flavour-filled heritage varieties on offer is particularly exciting. Chapters 4 and 5 will provide you with masses of ideas of different varieties to try.

Harvest gluts can become very boring; at first it is great fun having vegetables in abundance to offer neighbours and friends, but then eventually they too will be overwhelmed. When there is a glut of one particular vegetable, not only do you get tired of eating too much of it, even when it is at its freshest, but freezing or otherwise preserving it becomes a chore too. So small quantities, harvested over time, are best.

GROWING FOR HEALTH

We all know that eating vegetables and fruit is good for you, but one added bonus of growing your own is the exercise you will have digging and delving in and around your vegetable garden, helping to burn off calories and keep you in good shape.

The list of essential vitamins and minerals on the opposite page will help you decide which vegetables to grow.

▽ Herbs, fruit and edible flowers jostle with ornamentals for container space on a crowded, but productive roof terrace.

Vitamin A (antioxidant, good for the immune system and for night vision) is converted in the body from yellow-orange and red vegetables, and leafy greens including carrots, lettuce, parsley, peppers, spinach, squash and tomatoes.

Vitamin B (unlocks energy) is found in aubergines, broccoli, cauliflowers, courgettes, lettuce, parsley, peppers, squash and tomatoes.

Vitamin C (antioxidant, boosts immune system, protection against cancer and cardiovascular disease) is found in broccoli, Brussels sprouts, cabbages, cauliflowers, green beans, lettuce, parsley, peppers, potatoes, spinach and tomatoes.

Vitamin E (antioxidant) is found in green beans, peas and leafy greens.

Calcium (strengthening bones) is found in beans, broccoli, lettuce, parsley, peppers and tomatoes.

Iron (conductor of oxygen to cells) is found in lettuce, oriental greens, parsley, peas, spinach, and tomatoes.

Magnesium (nervous system) is found in beans, broccoli, cucumber, lettuce, peppers, potatoes, tomatoes, and squash.

Manganese (frees up proteins and fats) is found in beetroot, carrots, lettuce, peas and watercress.

Potassium (maintains fluids in cells) is found in aubergines, beans, broccoli, lettuce, carrots, cauliflowers, courgettes, cucumbers, oriental greens, parsley, peppers, radishes, spinach, squash and tomatoes.

Selenium (antioxidant, protects cells, boosts immune system) is found in beans, peas, sweetcorn and many other vegetables.

Zinc (DNA synthesis, cell division, growth) is found in beans, lettuce, parsley, peppers, potatoes, spinach and squash.

△ Every space in this enclosed garden has been used to good effect for productive and ornamental purposes. There is still room for a table and chairs to enable its owner to enjoy the garden's freshly picked harvest.

The demands of a small kitchen garden dictate that it must be as attractive as possible and yet also full and productive. There are a number of strategies for achieving this. Every space, no matter how small, is a planting opportunity.

getting
started

1

SMALL KITCHEN GARDENS
Sun, shade and shelter
Air circulation, Making a plan

ROOFTOPS AND BALCONIES
First considerations, Screening and shelter

PATIOS AND COURTYARDS
Practical pointers, Container gardens

IMPROVING THE SOIL
Preparation, Soil in containers,
Potting compost, Composting and
mulching, Wormeries, Watering

SOWING AND GROWING
Germination, Sowing in containers
Plant plugs, Successional planting

PESTS AND DISEASES
Common pests, Diseases

◁ A neat and functional layout with wide paths suits a small garden.

SMALL KITCHEN
gardens

If you are fortunate enough to have a garden, however small it may seem, you will be able to grow a good proportion of your own vegetables, herbs and fruit.

- SUN, SHADE AND SHELTER
  Providing shelter
- AIR CIRCULATION
- MAKING A PLAN

Most urban gardens are tucked away behind terraced or row houses and are of a roughly uniform shape and size. Long and narrow, with boundaries usually marked by fences or walls, they are in effect small outdoor living spaces, with varied demands put on the space by the different family members. If you are lucky enough to allocate as much as possible of the garden for vegetables you can plan for a traditional, albeit small-scale, row vegetable garden.

Even if you are only able to carve out a small square, rectangle or circle for the vegetable garden, it will still provide you with a range of fresh vegetables and fruits if you choose the varieties carefully and prepare the soil well. If you have to share your vegetable passions with other garden demands, it is likely that the area for vegetables will be to one side, with a wall or boundary of some sort, at the back of the site.

With a proper garden, you will be able to plant directly into the soil, unlike vegetable gardeners on rooftops and balconies, but you will have to prepare the soil well, especially if the garden has not been cultivated previously (see page 20). However, many small gardens suffer from the

GARDENER'S TIP
Use walls, arches or pergolas to support climbing plants, such as thornless blackberries or runner beans, to make most efficient use of space .

△ A small rectangular bed on a patio will provide a quantity of produce. Herbs, such as chives and parsley, offer light shade for a row of lettuces, while dwarf beans, sugar snap peas and broad beans planted in short rows are ready for harvest in early and midsummer.

effects of countless feet trampling them and compacting the soil. This will mean that it will be difficult to work the soil into a good state. The solution is to make raised beds (see page 34) filled with loam-based compost and well-rotted manure and leave to weather over the winter.

You will need a number of tools, some big and bulky such as hoses and lawn mowers, and others, such as forks and spades, that can be placed in specially designed store-cupboards, some of which double as garden benches. If you have the space for a small greenhouse or propagating unit, this will allow you to make sowings ahead of the warm weather.

SUN, SHADE AND SHELTER

When choosing where to site the vegetable plot, consider the garden as a whole.

• Track the sun and note the persistently shady areas of the site. Position the plot so all plants benefit from maximum sunshine and taller plants or climbing plants such as beans don't overshadow low-growing plants. Some vegetables and herbs thrive in shady conditions but the majority need the sun to make them grow and to

◁ If you have room, a small raised glasshouse is ideal for sowing early crops and for protecting tender herbs, such as basil, from frost.

△ All available space in this garden is well used. Fruit grows against the fence and archway, while borders and beds are filled with produce.

fill them with flavour and nutrients. Most vegetables need at least six hours per day in the sun. Lettuces and many salad leaves, as well as a few herbs, are the exception, preferring light shade.

• Also assess the site for shelter. Vegetables need open, sunny positions, but they also need shelter from drying and damaging winds.

• Pick a site where the vegetables are not competing with trees or hedges for the water and nutrients in the soil.

△ Good air circulation around plants helps to combat pests and diseases and makes it easier to weed and work between rows.

AIR CIRCULATION

Good air circulation is important for fertilization of some crops such as sweetcorn, and open airy sites will also be relatively pest and disease-free. However, strong wind is the vegetable grower's nightmare as it is the source of great stress for plants. Its action causes windrock, which in turn

loosens the root's grip on the soil, from where the plant derives its major source of vital water and nutrients. It also increases the rate at which plants lose water. This is a natural process, but if it happens too quickly, the plant will weaken and may collapse before it can replenish moisture levels.

Providing shelter To provide shelter, especially on rooftop gardens, patios and other exposed situations, you need to use lightweight material such as bamboo panels, which will look attractive when in place. Remember, though, that screening materials, however lightweight and non-competitive they may be, are likely to reduce light and moisture that would normally be available to the plants. Site screens carefully so that they don't shade the plants from their necessary daily quota of sunlight.

Hedges, while offering shelter, also compete with vegetable plants, so either you will have to provide plants with extra nutrition or use lightweight, man-made or natural materials.

MAKING A PLAN

1 Before planting up the plot, draw a sketch of your garden to scale and decide where the various beds, hedges, paths, seating and so on will be best placed.

2 Once the sketch is complete, mark its shape out on the ground, using pegs and string lines or with a line of sand, so that its actual position and size is apparent. Consider the layout from all angles and make any necessary adjustments .

3 Put in place the hard landscaping (paths, stepping stones, and so on) and the raised beds (wooden boards or brick-built beds), if relevant to the design.

4 Avoid compacting the soil by working on wooden boards laid over it to spread your weight.

◁ In this compact kitchen garden, paths are vital to provide access to the vegetables in the boarded, raised beds. They also add a pleasing visual neatness to the garden as a whole.

GARDENER'S TIP

If you are working on a new piece of ground which hasn't been cultivated before, you may need to remove turf and dig the ground. This is best done in autumn when the ground is still workable. Any compost or manure you work into it will also be well incorporated by the action of weather and the activity of soil organisms (see page 20).

▽ A rectangular shape divided by paths becomes a four-square garden. By siting the beds away from the hedges, you can access them easily.

▷ If you have cut beds from a previously turfed area, the ground needs to be well dug and compost or manure added to improve the soil's texture and fertility.

ROOFTOPS AND
balconies

If the only space for your vegetable garden is on a rooftop or balcony, a few practical challenges will need to be dealt with before you can start.

- FIRST CONSIDERATIONS
  Weight
  Surface material
  Sun and shade
  Drainage

- SCREENING AND SHELTER
  Wind protection

First of all, there will be no natural soil available and access to the roof or balcony will limit what you can transport, either with help or single-handedly. Whatever you need to get started – plants, soil, containers, decking and

propagators – has to fit into the lift or you need to be able to carry it. You may need to enlist help to get your roof or balcony garden going. Everything has to be transported up stairs or in lifts to the top of the building, in the case of roof gardens, or to a number of levels if the site is on a balcony. And on the return journey, any garden waste or debris has to come down in the same way and be disposed of safely.

Nonetheless, there is plenty of scope for growing vegetables in a wide variety of containers, and for adapting the space to house some permanent designed structures such as raised beds or decking. However, on rooftops these may be subject to planning permission and to structural constraints.

△ Hot peppers set tastebuds tingling and enliven the view from a balcony. They may need staking or shelter if the area is windy.

◁ The outer edges of a roof terrace are the strongest, weight-bearing areas. Even so, specially constructed wooden planters need to be carefully placed so they don't damage the flat roof.

FIRST CONSIDERATIONS

• **Weight** Before you begin a rooftop or balcony garden, make sure the structure can take the weight of the containers you are planning. On balconies and rooftops the outer edges are structurally the strongest areas, so it is wise to arrange containers around the edges. If you are able to construct raised beds (see page 34) to run around the boundaries of your roof or balcony space, this will be the safest option and will also provide the plants with the shelter of the adjacent walls.

• **Surface material** You will also need to take into consideration the material that covers the surface of the roof or balcony. Many flat roofs are sealed with tar which can become extremely hot in summer and large heavy pots will leave marks in it. A solution is to fit a raised decking over the whole or parts of the roof. This will keep the plants cooler in their pots and will mean that the roof surface is not damaged.

• **Sun and shade** Just as for a ground level garden, you need to track the sun and establish where the shade is and where the hot-spots are.

• **Drainage** On balconies you will need to consider the neighbours downstairs when you are watering the containers. A muddy waterfall spilling from your balcony to another will not

endear you to your neighbours. As far as it is possible, only water directly into the containers and place water-holding saucers under pots.

SCREENING AND SHELTER

City rooftops and balconies on different levels provide limited spaces with great views. Like country landowners, city gardeners on high levels can 'borrow the landscape' around them. These potential growing sites are usually facing similar balconies and rooftops that return the gaze and see your balcony as 'the view', so you may feel that you need the privacy offered by screening.

• **Wind protection** Rooftops and balconies are notoriously windy so the screening will also help to make the site more sheltered for your plants. Exposure to wind can be reduced by using lightweight screening material and growing the climbing plants on it to get maximum value out of every bit of space. Many rooftop spaces are enclosed by walls on several sides and these can be used to support lightweight netting systems to hold beans and peas which will thrive in such sheltered positions, as well as lower-growing plants such as tomatoes, peppers and potatoes.

△ Even on the smallest rooftop there is the opportunity to grow a range of vegetables in attractive containers. Individual kohlrabi plants will be replaced by more of the same, or a different crop, such as lettuces.

◁ A glass screen offers permanent shelter on a windy balcony, yet does not reduce light levels. In addition, it provides a private spot to enjoy in apple blossom time, as well as at other times through the year.

PATIOS AND
courtyards

In terms of spaces and shapes, patios and courtyards present the same sort of challenges as balconies and roof gardens. The difference is that at ground level, there isn't the worry about weight and the need to transport everything upwards.

- PRACTICAL POINTERS
    Access
    Aspect
    Raised beds

- CONTAINER GARDENS

PRACTICAL POINTERS

• **Access** The consideration of access remains a key factor, especially if the only access to the courtyard or patio is through the house and not by means of a side entrance. If you plan to include a large structure, such as a garden bench or an arch, either choose a flat-packed style or measure doorways or narrow passageways carefully first.

• **Aspect** Patios and courtyards are often shaded by neighbouring or opposing buildings, only receiving sun in the middle of the day. However, surrounding buildings will also offer shelter and this can protect the site from frost and wind. You can also increase the light and warmth of the patio and courtyard space by painting walls white to reflect the sun.

• **Raised beds** As these areas are often paved or have a concrete floor, growing in raised beds or containers is the solution (see pages 34 and 42). Once you have overcome the logistical difficulties of balconies, rooftops, patios and

△ Beans and tomatoes provide attractive foliage, colourful flowers and tasty fruits, and make a pleasing counterpoint for low-growing bedding plants.

◁ A raised platform on a patio doubles as a planting area and is framed by a row of herbs and salad leaves with pots of herbs and beans running the length of tiered staging.

courtyards, you will find many opportunities for using containers inventively, and decorative as well as productive plantings will be limitless.

CONTAINER GARDENS

On a rooftop, balcony or patio you won't need to draw a paper layout of the site, but the same principles apply.

• Sit down on the patio or roof garden and see which areas are the sunniest, where the prevailing wind is and work out where to place climbing plants and containers for salads so that they benefit from the best available positions.

• You may well wish to make a sketch highlighting the different containers that you plan to use and to draw up a planting checklist.

• It is unlikely that you will have a greenhouse so you may need an indoor site for seed sowing. If you do have the space on the roof garden or patio for a tall shelved seed-sowing unit, you will be able to raise many of your own plants.

△ Small and sunny, the density of planting within this enclosed courtyard makes it appear much larger than it is. The formality of its framework adds to the sense of size and containers set on the gravel beds offer extra planting sites.

▽ A productive climbing gourd grows overs the fencing in this sheltered, plant-enclosed patio, where vegetables and nasturtiums mingle with ornamental plants, such as shaped box in containers.

IMPROVING
the soil

The soil, and its health, are of paramount importance to the quality of the food and the quantity of the yield you are likely to produce in your kitchen garden.

• PREPARATION
  Soil types

• SOIL IN CONTAINERS

• POTTING COMPOST
  Loam-based compost, Soilless compost

• COMPOSTING AND MULCHING

• WORMERIES

• WATERING

PREPARATION

Autumn is the best time to prepare the site. Soil that has not previously been used for vegetable growing needs double-digging to aerate and open it up. If possible, you should also dig in well-rotted manure and home-made bulky organic compost (see page 22). These elements will enrich the soil and encourage the activity of micro-organisms and beneficial insects and invertebrates. There are some vegetable crops such as potatoes that will be good to grow in previously uncultivated soil. You can also improve the soil's overall fertility by applying chemical fertilizers, by growing and digging in green manures and by adding bulky organic matter to the soil when you dig it over in autumn.

Soil types There are four types of soil – sandy, loam, clay and chalk – and each has different attributes and will support a range of vegetables. However, to grow a wider variety in a particular soil you may need to improve or change your existing soil. A slightly acid soil with average fertility and a high organic content will satisfy the widest choice of fruits and vegetables.

• Light, free-draining soils are very useful for producing early crops but because of their structure they lose nutrients and moisture quickly. You can improve this by adding a standard fertilizer and working in organic matter when you dig the soil in autumn.

• Heavy clay soils are either too wet or too dry. In wet periods they become sticky and water-

△ A well-balanced soil that has been dug over in autumn with compost added will provide the perfect environment for a wide range of home-grown vegetables.

logged, while in hot dry periods they crack. In spring they are cold and take longer than a sandy soil to warm up. In time you can improve them by adding abundant organic material, horticultural grit and sharp sand.

For high yields, soil needs to have an open, aerated structure and it should hold moisture and nutrients for the roots. First and foremost, keep off the soil yourself. You can do this by growing vegetables in raised beds or beds that you can work from the sides, rather than walk on the plot itself. If you have to walk on the soil, use wooden boards so that you don't compact the soil.

SOIL IN CONTAINERS

It is best to use a proprietary potting compost where the nutrient level and structure is measurable, as opposed to digging up soil from the garden. In the garden plants will be able to reach and use the available nutrients and moisture, but once garden soil is used in a container it is difficult to quantify the amount of nutrient and there may be deficiencies or diseases. To make sure your container vegetables are receiving their nutrient quota you will have to provide it in the

form of liquid fertilizers or through slow-release fertilizers added at the time of potting up.

POTTING COMPOST

There are two types of compost, loam-based and soilless, each with its good and bad points.

Loam-based compost will support a good range of food plants. However, it is heavier in weight than soilless compost, which can be problematic on balconies and roofs and may make it very difficult to move containers around easily.

Using a weightier compost can be an advantage, provided the roof can cope with the additional weight, as loam-based compost does provide stability in the pot for the plants. It releases nutrients over time, is free-draining and

△ To keep the soil in good health, avoid walking directly on it. Use wooden boards as temporary walkways between rows, so that you can work from them. They will also suppress weeds.

◁ It is relatively easy to improve the soil if you grow vegetables in raised beds. You can add soil and compost to the bed, to the height of the boards of the raised bed's sides.

▷ Compost is one of the garden's most precious harvests. Following the small-space principles of ornament and beauty, camouflage a plastic compost bin with a wooden hurdle and a wigwam of sweet peas.

▽ The soil conditioner here is home-made compost produced in a tumbling composter. Held above the ground on a metal frame, the bin is turned frequently so the material inside is well-mixed.

has a good structure. All this makes for good establishment of healthy productive plants but has to be set against the weight factor.

Soilless compost Peat is the main ingredient of soilless compost. Other materials include grit, shredded bark or coir and vermiculite, all of which improve the drainage. It is lighter than loam-based compost, but is less stable. It is not as moisture-retentive, so when a soilless compost dries out it is difficult to re-wet it satisfactorily.

COMPOSTING AND MULCHING

If you have space, install a compost bin or make a small area of the garden into a compost site.

• Place the compost bin, usually made out of plastic, on well-drained soil in a sunny site, close to the vegetable plot.

• Add any kitchen vegetable and fruit peelings (high in nitrogen and carbon), tea leaves, coffee

grounds, crushed eggshells, prunings from other plants, and vacuum-cleaner dust.

• If you have garden waste such as weeds (as long as the seeds are not ripe), evergreen clippings or leaves, you can add these as well.

• You should not include any diseased plant material, cooked food (it will attract rodents) or the faeces of domestic pets.

• Add different types of material in layers and from time to time add activators or accelerators that will add nitrogen to the heap and heat up the compost so that it decomposes more quickly. There are natural activators, such as uric acid, farmyard manure, seaweed, comfrey and grass clippings, as well as many commercial activators available in liquid or powder form. You may not need to add an activator, but in colder weather or winter it will help to speed up the process.

• Keep the lid on your compost heap or cover it with a piece of old carpet to retain heat and moisture and to protect it from rain. If the compost become very dry, add sufficient water to moisten

it (but don't saturate it). For example, a heap or bin 30–60 cm (1–2 ft) in depth may need several large watering cans.

• The compost is ready to use when it has changed into a friable, crumbly mixture that resembles the proprietary compost blends available from garden centres. You will be able to dig this into your containers and into the garden or use it as a mulch around plants.

Mulching (covering the surface of the soil with straw, compost, bark or leaf mould) reduces water loss from the soil surface, keeps it warmer and lessens annual weed germination rates.

WORMERIES

It will be difficult to keep a successful compost bin going in the limited space of a balcony or a roof garden, but if you have the space a wormery will provide liquid fertilizer as well as friable compost. Wormeries take up a small amount of space and can be fixed to a wall. They are relatively clean and easy to assemble and use. Green-fingered children are likely to be very good caretakers of the whole system.

A wormery is a unit of stacking or tiered containers used to house a collection of worms which will turn kitchen waste into compost. The worms will eat their own weight of waste each day transforming it into a concentrated liquid fertiliser and a solid, soil-improving compost. The liquid can be drained off daily once the wormery is established and used, diluted, according to the instructions that accompany the wormery. The highly nutritious solid material can be used to improve the soil. Keep the wormery in a frost-free site during the winter.

WATERING

For convenience, the site needs good access to watering facilities. If necessary, think about laying in an irrigation system which can be computerized or automated. This can be a large investment but it

will pay off in the long term. In a container vegetable garden on a roof or patio, a watering system can be invaluable, especially if timed to come on and off several times a day to give plants regular watering. Plants take up water from the soil in the ground or in containers through their roots and in hot periods or when seedlings are establishing it is vital to add to the reserves of water in the soil.

Whether you grow vegetables in containers or in the ground, always make sure you water the ground or the potting medium, rather than the whole plant. Keep a reservoir of water in a plant saucer, under the plants in containers and whatever you do, avoid spraying over the leaves. In sunlight this will result in leaf scorch.

△ In a traditional row garden it is feasible to install an under-soil, computerized watering system. Water is available in the soil at chosen times, and although it might at first seem to use more water than a conventional hosepipe, no water is wasted on plant foliage.

> ### GARDENER'S TIP
> *To prevent compost drying out in containers, mix water-retaining gel or granules into the potting medium before you plant up the containers.*

SOWING AND growing

Sowing your own seeds and watching your vegetables and herbs growing from small seedlings can be very satisfying, but you will need to plan ahead and have patience.

- GERMINATION
- SOWING IN CONTAINERS
- PLANT PLUGS
- SUCCESSIONAL PLANTING

GERMINATION

Seeds need warmth to germinate. Most seed packets will give an indication of when you should sow seeds direct into the ground, but remember that this is a general instruction and you should always make an adjustment for your particular micro-climate. If you can sow seed indoors to get a head start, don't start too early or you will be inundated with seedlings which will soon become leggy if it is still too cold to plant them outside.

Most vegetable seeds can be sown directly into the ground, but many half-hardy plants, such as tomatoes, aubergines, cucumbers and basil, will need to be started off in a propagator or on a warm sunny windowsill. In general they will need a temperature of 10–21°C (50–70°F) in order to germinate. You will need to keep a sunny windowsill in action during the year if you are sowing in succession and need replacements for vegetables as they are harvested.

Carrots, beetroot, parsnips and radishes can be sown directly into the ground or into containers and you can thin out as they mature.

SOWING IN CONTAINERS

1 Use containers such as seed trays or cellular sowing trays and fill them almost to the top with soilless compost.
2 Flatten the surface with a piece of board, then moisten the compost using a watering can with a fine rose or a mist sprayer filled with water.

△ You can sow pumpkins and courgettes direct into their growing sites, but you can extend the growing season by sowing them indoors so they are ready to plant out as soon as all danger of frost is over.

3 Sow fine seed thinly onto the surface of the compost and barely cover with a layer of compost, sow larger seed deeper into the compost. If you are using a cellular tray, sow one or two seeds into each cell. Cover large seeds such as tomatoes with compost.

4 Place the newly sown seed trays in a propagator or cover them with a polythene bag and place on a sunny windowsill. Check the compost regularly but don't overwater.

5 Once the seeds have germinated, remove the propagator lid or polythene bag. When the seedlings are growing strongly, bring them into more direct light and water to keep the compost just moist.

6 When the seedlings have grown large enough to handle you can prick them out into larger pots. You may need to harden them off – put them outside during the day and bring them indoors at night until they have adjusted to the outside temperature.

If you have sown seed into cellular sowing trays or other small containers, wait until two true seed leaves are showing and the seedlings are

PLANT PLUGS

Many seed companies offer individual seedlings and small plants each grown in a tiny 'plug' of compost. The range offered is wide, and these young plants are ideal for gardeners who don't have a greenhouse or propagator. It could be argued that on their journey through the mail to you they will have endured root disturbance, but by the time they reach you they will have gone through all the difficult stages in a young plant's life and are less likely to suffer from damping off (the fungal disease which can wipe out a whole collection of seedlings soon after germination). They will establish quickly once you plant them into their growing sites.

Plant plugs are usually accompanied by growing instructions, but the most important step is to remove them from their packaging and, if they need water, apply it carefully and sparsely and plant them up as soon as possible. Orders are usually despatched to coincide with the correct time for you to plant out.

just large enough for you to handle before you plant them into their growing positions. Handle gently as any damage will result in a shock to the plant's system and a setback in its growth.

SUCCESSIONAL PLANTING

Successional planting is a useful technique that helps to extend the growing season. Staggered sowing or planting of vegetables such as lettuce which, if sown in one go will all come to readiness at one time, is the key to success. As one crop matures and is harvested, another is well on its way to replace it. Gardeners describe this as 'sowing a little and often'. This method requires a series of 'under-study' plants, waiting in the wings, ready to take centre stage when the current plant has been harvested.

△ Harden off seedlings sown indoors by gradually acclimatizing them to outdoor conditions in a coldframe over a period of days. Make mini-greenhouses from cutaway plastic bottles, which will provide frost protection for young plants.

PESTS AND
diseases

All plants in all gardens – whether cultivated at ground level or higher up, in beds or in containers – are likely to suffer from pests and diseases at some stage in their development.

- COMMON PESTS
  A–Z directory

- DISEASES
  A–Z directory

- CROP ROTATION

The cleaner you can keep your tools, the site and your pots, the lower the chances are for devastating infections or pest problems. Whether you use alternative or mainstream chemical sprays to control pests and diseases, make sure you read the manufacturer's instructions and follow them carefully. There are many alternative treatments available and you can also select vegetable varieties which are resistant to particular pests and diseases, minimizing the chance of infection.

There are also some useful techniques like companion planting of flowers that will attract predatory and pollinating insects which will have a beneficial effect on the pest situation. Many gardeners use French marigolds inter-planted with tomatoes and brassicas, the poached egg plant *(Limnanthes douglasii)* and fennel, to attract hoverflies which control garden pests.

There are numerous protective materials such as netting for covering soft fruit bushes to guard the fruit against birds. Some gardeners use stylish scarecrows or make their own bird-scarers. There are black cat faces with glowing eyes which can be inserted into vegetable rows or into containers to imitate cats and thus ward off birds. Humming lines (plastic tapes which, when pulled taut between canes, make a sound to deter birds) are also useful and in some high-tech gardens unwanted CDs are strung onto lengths of wire or string and recycled as glinting bird-scarers.

△ Coloured ties and old CDs which glint in the sunlight are among the unusual and inventive measures adopted by gardeners to keep birds off vegetable crops.

COMMON PESTS

APHIDS

Greenfly and blackfly are different types of aphid. They damage plants by clustering on stems, leaves and buds and sucking the sap of the plants. They can overwhelm plants or simply cause distortion to stems and shoots and may also bring virus infections with them.

• They can be removed and crushed by hand (wear gloves if you are squeamish).

• Otherwise, dislodge them with strong blast of water, or spray with a solution of insecticidal soap.

• Natural predators include ladybirds, which are drawn in by their presence, and hoverflies which are attracted by fennel flowers and poached egg plants.

CABBAGE ROOT FLY

This fly's maggots attack the roots of all brassicas including kohlrabi, kales and broccoli, boring into the roots. It is at the seedling or transplant stage that the crop is most vulnerable.

• Protect the plants with barriers such as special brassica collars on the ground at the plant's base or a covering of horticultural fleece until the plants are well established.

△ Porous horticultural fleece, which doesn't affect light levels, seems to deter the cabbage root fly from damaging the plant's roots at seedling stage.

CARROT FLY

The maggots of this fly attack carrot, parsnip and celery roots. The fly is attracted by the smell of the foliage when it is crushed, so if you thin the seedlings or weed around them, this is sure to attract the pest.

• Avoid the need to thin by spacing seed further apart at sowing time.

• Use carrot fly-resistant varieties, such as 'Fly Away'.

• Erect a barrier of plastic or fleece that is at least 75 cm (30 in) high.

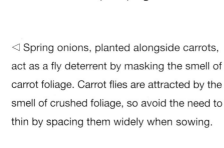

◁ Spring onions, planted alongside carrots, act as a fly deterrent by masking the smell of carrot foliage. Carrot flies are attracted by the smell of crushed foliage, so avoid the need to thin by spacing them widely when sowing.

CATERPILLARS

Caterpillars eat the foliage of many plants and can be picked off by hand.
• Check the foliage, especially on the undersides, for the caterpillars.
• Also check the undersides of the leaves for eggs and squash these.

FLEA BEETLES

Flea beetles damage the foliage of many vegetable plants, including brassicas and peas, making small holes and weakening, even overwhelming seedlings. Healthy, strong plants are not as susceptible.
• Sow in good conditions so seedlings can establish.
• Cover the crop with a fleece barrier.

△ Cabbage-white caterpillars.

ONION FLY

Onions, leeks and shallots are vulnerable to the maggots of this fly which will bore into the bulbs and stems.
• Crop rotation (see page 29) minimizes the chances of onion fly spreading.
• In addition, try to grow your onion crop from sets rather than from seed, as they are less likely to be affected than seed-raised onions (see page 61).

RED SPIDER MITE

The symptoms are small yellow and white markings and webbing on leaves. They are prevalent in hot, dry greenhouses and may be more of a problem for container-grown vegetables than in the ground.
• In greenhouses, use predatory mites, *Phytoseiulus persimilis.*
• In the open and in containers make sure plants are well-watered in dry periods, if necessary misting the foliage of container-grown plants in the evening or when they are in the shade.

SLUGS AND SNAILS

These invertebrates damage the foliage and young shoots of most vegetables, including lettuces and brassicas.
• They are large enough to be picked off and removed by hand.
• There are other barrier methods such as crushed egg shells, gravel and other uneven, sharp materials that can be placed around the plants to deter the slugs and snails.
• Slug pubs – a dish, yoghurt carton or specially bought container – can be filled with some leftover beer, the smell of which attracts the slugs, which fall in and drown.

△ Hoverflies are predators of aphids.

VINE WEEVILS

Vegetables cultivated in the ground are not likely to be attacked by vine weevils, but if you use soilless compost for vegetables grown in containers, check it for fat white grubs.
• Remove and destroy any you find (do not throw them on the compost heap).
• You are less likely to encounter this pest in loam-based compost, although fruit grown in containers is susceptible.
• Use nematodes to control them outdoors in spring and autumn.

DISEASES

APPLE AND PEAR CANKER

The symptoms of canker are distorted sections of wood and black patches that appear on the skin of fruits.
• Control by pruning out affected sections of wood.
• Remove and destroy the damaged fruits.
• Choose the modern canker-resistant varieties and improve soil drainage.

BLIGHT (potato and tomato)

This affects potatoes and outdoor tomatoes. It is most likely to occur in damp, humid weather and can damage the plants very quickly.

• Use resistant varieties.

• Improve the air circulation around the crop by increasing planting distances.

• Always remove any affected plants, and dispose of them or burn them.

CLUBROOT

This organism affects brassica roots, resulting in weak, unhealthy, stunted plants.

• Avoid it by rotating crops.

• Lime the soil (always follow manufacturer's instructions).

• For a small planting of brassicas add ericaceous compost to the planting trench. This will increase the acidity, which brassicas prefer and as it is fresh, is less likely to harbour the organism.

• Always dispose of affected plants.

DAMPING OFF

Poor hygiene, including the use of rain water and old compost, results in this fungal attack which may overwhelm young seedlings and plants. Signs of it include the stems rotting and turning black and the plant dying off.

• Only use water straight from the tap and always use fresh compost for seed sowing and transplanting.

• Sowing the seeds too close together can also encourage damping off.

DOWNY MILDEW

This fungal disease shows as a fluffy, shadowy outline on leaves of brassicas, lettuce and onions.

• Make sure there is good air circulation around plants.

• Remove any affected parts and keep the area weed-free.

GREY MOULD

Poor hygiene and cool, damp growing conditions will increase the likelihood of grey mould occurring on above-ground parts of the plant.

• Remove affected plants (or just the affected parts of them).

• Don't wet foliage when watering.

POWDERY MILDEW

Courgettes and brassicas, amongst other plants, are susceptible to powdery mildew, which is prevalent in dry weather. A white fungal growth appears on the upper leaf surfaces.

• Water regularly in dry periods.

• Improve air circulation and good garden hygiene to avoid it.

RUSTS

Leeks are prone to rust, which appears as bright orange spores on the leaves.

• Remove badly infected parts of the plant, and clear away.

• Keep water off the leaves.

• Improve hygiene.

SILVER LEAF

This disease affects stone fruits such as cherries, plums and greengages. It occurs if the wood is damaged or pruned at the wrong time.

• Summer pruning reduces the chance of the tree succumbing to it.

VIRUSES

Viruses affect many vegetables such as cucumbers, courgettes and marrows and result in stunted unhealthy plants.

• Choose resistant varieties.

• Destroy affected plants as disease will spread through to others in the row.

CROP ROTATION

In a small space you might be tempted to grow the same crop in the same place year on year. However, this is likely to lead to a build up of the pests and diseases that affect the particular crop in that part of the garden. Crop rotation can be a useful method. The basic principle is that you divide the available space into four sections and move the vegetables according to the group they come under into another section each year, in a four-year cycle.

1 Vegetables in the first group are the legumes and include peas, beans, and all plants with podded fruits. Sweetcorn is also included.

2 Brassicas, including broccoli, cabbages, cauliflowers and kale, make up the second group.

3 The third group includes root vegetables such as beetroot, carrots, parsnips, potatoes and turnips. Include tomatoes and peppers too.

4 The fourth group is the onion tribe which includes shallots, leeks, garlic and chives. You can include courgettes in this section as well.

If you are not growing brassicas, ignore them as a group and simply divide the area into three sections and rotate three groups over a three-year period.

The way you plan your vegetable garden will depend on the space available; there are many ways to get the most out of small spaces. Whether you grow vegetables in traditional rows or in the flower borders, the results will be productive and ornamental.

garden
layouts

2

TRADITIONAL ROWS
Advantages, Short rows and blocks
Wide rows, Close spacing
Intercropping

RAISED BEDS
Practicalities, Soil
Four-square gardening

DECORATIVE PLANTING
Dual-purpose planting
Potagers, Colour scheming
Climbing plants

PATHS AND WALKWAYS
Paths, Bed edgings

◁ In this garden, early vegetables, such as broad beans and lettuces, will be harvested before crops such as celery need more of the space.

TRADITIONAL rows

Linear or straight rows of produce are the traditional choice in most vegetable gardens, and may be the best solution for maximum use of the available ground.

- ADVANTAGES
  Calculating space
- SHORT ROWS AND BLOCKS
- WIDE ROWS
- CLOSE SPACING
- INTERCROPPING

△ In a traditional vegetable row each crop is grown in a long line, with regular spacing between rows. It is easy to keep rows weed-free by hoeing down the lines.

ADVANTAGES

It is simplest to sow seed into straight rows and, as a general rule, rows are easier to maintain. Weeding is easier if plants are all growing in one axis as the weeds can be easily identified and hoed off. It is also more convenient to water along rows without wetting foliage and if you need to warm up the soil or protect plants, standard cloches are more likely to fit the average row.

Calculating space Traditional row-growing needs more space than other systems, and produces more of a particular crop. In the row system you need to have space between rows and between plants within the rows and it is these requirements that take up the space. The minimum space between rows is 15 cm (6 in), the maximum is 45 cm (18 in), depending on whether the vegetables are small, large or greedy feeders which need more space. However, there are many other ways to divide the space, or rather, to manage and arrange the vegetables.

SHORT ROWS AND BLOCKS

You don't have to fill a long row with just one type of vegetable – you can split rows and in a long thin town garden, short rows, where you sow vegetables in blocks of several short rows, may work best. This also looks attractive, as you have sections with different shapes, colours and textures of vegetables. And it means that you can make repeat or successional sowings at a future point in time.

WIDE ROWS

Wide row planting is a system favoured by many American gardeners, including Californian garden writer Rosalind Creasey, author of *Edible Landscaping*. In this system rows about 1 m (3 ft) wide and 5 m (15 ft) long are either dug into the ground or are contained in a raised bed (see page 34). The long wide bed can be worked from the paths and edible flowering plants are used as companions to make the garden look attractive, to aid pollination and also to use in salads.

CLOSE SPACING

Mini or baby vegetables widely available in supermarkets are 'designer' crops, small enough to provide the flavour of their full-size relatives and fun to grow in containers and small urban gardens. They can be grown by planting ordinary varieties very close together and picking them before they fully mature. There are also many varieties that have dwarfing characteristics or have been bred to produce mini-versions of their larger mainstream relations (see page 66).

INTERCROPPING

Intercropping is another way of getting the most out of a small space. This technique is used in any intensive cropping system and involves combining crops which have differing growing times. Carrots and parsnips will take longer to reach maturity than radishes which can be successfully inter-cropped with them, that is planted in the spaces between rows of carrots and parsnips. The radishes will be ready to harvest ahead of the carrots, and by the time the carrots are getting larger, and needing more of the nutrients and moisture available, the radishes will be out of the ground. The intercropping regime can continue with, for example, a sowing of lettuce into the space left by the radishes.

△ By intercropping vegetables and herbs, such as leeks with parsley, it is possible to use limited space even more productively.

△ Even in a traditional row layout, many vegetables, such as lettuces, can be grown successfully when closely planted.

▷ Close planting looks very attractive and by harvesting alternate plants you can prolong the display.

RAISED
beds

Defining the vegetable garden's limits with raised beds provides small spaces that are useful for maximum cropping and ideal for courtyard or rooftop gardens.

- PRACTICALITIES
- SOIL
- FOUR-SQUARE GARDENING

PRACTICALITIES

Raised beds can be brick-built or have their sides enclosed with wooden boards or railway sleepers. With this method, the soil is effectively raised above ground level. Good organic material can be worked in. In these small spaces, plants may still be arranged in rows, but planting distances are reduced, keeping weeds in check and allowing you to produce more plants. You could also adopt any of the other bed layouts suggested in this chapter.

SOIL

The soil within the raised bed needs to be dug over and prepared well (see page 20), then additional material from the compost heap (if

△ Raised beds can be edged with boards, railway sleepers or, as shown here, with brick. This provides a permanent feature and offers ease of access for both maintenance and harvesting.

◁ Within a raised bed system it is possible to grow vegetables and herbs at a high density. As you pick, the remaining plants spread to fill the spaces and can be grown on for a later harvest.

you have one) is added. The width of the raised bed is critical: any wider than 90 cm (36 in) and it will not be possible to work the centre without stepping onto the soil. And that is the whole point of this gardening system – it doesn't need the space between vegetable rows for walking on or working from. This means the soil will not be damaged or compacted by you and if enriched regularly with compost, will go on producing healthy, tasty vegetables over a long period.

▷ Raised beds are particularly useful on patios or courtyards where a reasonable depth of a workable soil is otherwise difficult to achieve. Here an attractive log edging provides a decorative touch.

FOUR-SQUARE GARDENING

This is a technique devised by American vegetable gardener Mel Bartholomew for growing many crops in small spaces. The basic size of the area is a square 1.2 x 1.2 m (4 x 4 ft). The square is further divided into sixteen 30 cm (1 ft) squares. Make yourself a grid system with string or wires laid across the large square. Each small square is used for a different crop, or you can use several squares for a particular crop. This gives an attractive patchwork effect. In production terms it enables you to grow many more plants and the basic shape will fit into a small garden. The square is enclosed by four wooden sides, so becomes a raised bed which you fill with a mix of garden compost, potting compost and vermiculite. Each time a square is harvested, replenish the compost to refresh the soil and plant another crop. The planting is carefully managed so the tallest crops are grown at the back or on the north side of the bed and don't shade the lower crops. This means all the plants get the same amount of sunlight. Giant vegetables aren't possible in this system but you will get a crop of tasty smaller vegetables, and weed and pest control is easy from the sides.

BACK ROW
• **Sugar snap peas** 'Oregon Sugarpod' or
• **Runner beans** 'Prize Winner'. Use all four small squares to ensure a reasonable harvest.

SECOND ROW
• **Kohlrabi** 'Purple Delicacy': four plants.
• **Onion** sets (either 16 for smaller onions or nine for larger onions).
• **Lamb's lettuce** can be sown later on direct into the square for a winter salad crop.
• **Beetroot** 'Monogram' (either 16 for small beets or nine for larger individual beetroot).
• **Leeks** 'King Richard'.

THIRD ROW
• **Dwarf runner bean** 'Hestia'.
• **Carrot** 'Parmex' or 'Early Nantes': broadcast the seed or sow in three rows and thin out.
• **Turnip** 'Milan Purple Top' (sow in two rows or broadcast over the square).

• **Dwarf French beans**: four plants, 'Purple Teepee' or 'Royalty'.

FRONT ROW
• **Parsley**: either plant in nine small pots for a full look, broadcast or plant in three rows.
• **Lettuce** 'Little Gem' or 'Red Salad Bowl': sow into three rows or transplant 16 seedlings or young plants.
• **Roquette** broadcast seed over the square or sow into three rows.
• **Cut-and-come-again lettuce**: sow into three rows.

DECORATIVE planting

In a small garden, where the vegetable plot is on show, it is important to make the beds look as attractive as possible. There are several different ways you can achieve this. The following ideas can be used in raised beds or at ground level.

- DUAL-PURPOSE PLANTING
  Edgings
  Beans and peas
  Hedges and dividers
  Soft fruit

- POTAGERS

- COLOUR SCHEMING

- CLIMBING PLANTS

DUAL-PURPOSE PLANTING

In row-gardening (the slightly disparaging name given to traditional vegetable gardens), the plants thrive in long lines, are harvested and the ground then lies fallow, waiting for the next crop. In small space gardening, the rows are turned into decoration, with planting blocks in short rows or in squares grown in ever-diminishing squares within each other. This is essentially growing in rows, but rows with a difference.

• **Edgings** In the same way, you can grow a crop, such as parsley, lettuce, chives or even leeks, as the double-duty decorative and pro-ductive edging for a bed of other vegetables. Keep the row attractive when you harvest by replacing with new plants or by harvesting in a sequence, say of every other plant. In this way the decorative edge won't disappear all at once.

• **Beans and peas** can be used to provide temporary cover or screening on a patio or a roof garden. Bean flowers are attractive and peas and beans in pod offer a wide range of colour combinations, as well as tastes after harvesting.

• **Hedges and dividers** Think even bigger and turn hedges into productive plantings. Fruit trees, such as apples and pears, can be trained into architectural shapes, so that they fulfil a structural function as well as a productive one. For example, step-over apples (see page 71), at just 45 cm (18 in) high, provide a boundary marker for the fruit and vegetable garden but also provide both produce and ornament.

△ Here the colourful foliage of cabbages and lettuces combine with that of golden and green box plants to make a dazzling ornamental display. The productive qualities of the plants are secondary to the aesthetics, although by the time the cabbages need more space the lettuces will have been harvested.

▷ Many vegetables look attractive in a border. Here runner beans add height and lettuces have been left to set seed. Although the lettuces are too bitter at this stage to harvest, they still offer colour and shape.

• **Soft fruit** can also be grown for a dual purpose. Choose standard gooseberries for height and shape, as well as their fruits. Use thornless blackberries on fences or arches, or grow blueberries and figs in containers on a patio or balcony.

POTAGERS

Colourful flowers, attractive foliage and bright fruits are among the decorative attributes of many vegetables. Ornamental vegetable gardening now has a great following. Described as potagers, these gardens combine production with aesthetics. Usually arranged within small formal, box-edged beds, the vegetables are chosen for their visual attractions and the overall effect is of a tapestry of texture and colour. They are also combined with flowers and shrubs.

Among my choices here are some of the cabbage family which I would normally consider too large to be worthwhile in the small space kitchen

△ Two apple trees specially trained to form a low hedge provide the small garden with a productive and attractive definition within a box-hedged frame.

garden. These include red kale 'Redbor' which, with its deeply indented and striking red-purple foliage, makes a dramatic border plant.

COLOUR SCHEMING

You can choose vegetables primarily for their taste, but the colour and texture of their leaves and the shapes in which they grow, are factors in the mix. Lettuce, providing crunch and crispy texture, whether planted in rows or in containers, comes in a rainbow wave of wonderful colours, from bright apple-green through to translucent pinks and purple. Chard, whose stems and leaves are delicious simply blanched and brushed with butter, is available in white-, yellow- and red-stemmed and veined forms, all of which

are striking. Beetroot foliage, delicious when young in salads, comes in a green and purple veined combination as well as in a matt purple.

CLIMBING PLANTS

Climbing and vining plants, such as beans, peas, grapes and some squash and gourds, need support. In the small space garden this offers you another opportunity to use the vegetables for that extra double-duty of ornament and function. For some plants such as pumpkin and squash this may be the only way that you can include these space-eaters. Gourds are naturally vining and, if offered upward support, will scramble up and cling to an archway or other strong structure.

• Metal arches are suitably strong supports for heavier plants such as grape vines, thornless blackberries and pumpkin or squash vines.

• Formal structural garden features such as wooden or iron obelisks can be used to support vegetable climbers but when covered in beans or vines, their own intrinsic structural impact will be hidden from view.

• Supports for beans are usually in the shape of a framework of canes arranged either in long, double rows, with canes crossing and secured at the top with canes running the length of the row, or round, wigwam arrangements of canes. However there are variations and the canes can be arranged as uprights, with string wound between them to support the bean plants as they grow. Try rustic sticks or poles as an alternative.

• Peas will also need support but shorter canes or a series of woody branches hung with pea netting will be sufficient.

GARDENER'S TIP

Use climbing vegetable plants, such as runner beans, to provide shade and privacy on a roof garden. Train the beans over a simple framework of canes.

△ Beans and other climbing vegetables need a framework. In the small garden this can be achieved using many different attractive support systems.

▷ If there is not enough space to grow pumpkin and squash on the ground, provide plants with a strong metal or wooden support, such as an iron archway or an old climbing frame, and they will happily scramble upwards.

PATHS AND
walkways

If the vegetable garden is to be divided into small sectors, it is important to decide how you want to access each individual section for planting, weeding, watering and harvesting the crops.

- PATHS
    Stepping stones
- BED EDGINGS

PATHS

Garden paths can be made from a wide variety of materials including gravel, sand, bark chippings or pavers. Old bricks in mellow, weathered colours can be laid in a traditional herringbone pattern, while slate chips look attractive and very modern. The simplest paths consist of straw or bark chippings, laid directly onto the soil. You can make the layers as thick as the available straw or bark chippings will allow. It will be 'walked' around and flung about the garden by birds, but is easily reconsolidated.

Stepping stones can be placed into the planting area, so that you can get straight into the garden to work. If possible try to keep off the soil so that you don't compact it, making it impervious to water. This will mean that water doesn't drain away well, so roots will not have even access to water and young plants may be swamped by too much water at their necks.

BED EDGINGS

Natural materials are also useful to make decorative edges for the vegetable garden, separating the beds from the paths. They take up very little space and yet offer definition to the garden. Choose materials to complement the paths. For example, if the path is made from bark chippings, twiggy pieces of curved willow stems become a lightweight barrier, to keep plants off paths and people off the plants. Hazel twigs woven together offer a similar effect.

△ Stepping stones placed at intervals across a vegetable garden provide access and still leave much of the soil free for planting.

▷ Slate chippings laid onto a well-constructed path offer extra and often complementary colour for ornament.

△ The boards that enclose a raised bed help to keep the leaves at the edge of the planting off the ground, as well as hold the path material off the soil.

◁ Gravel is a popular material for paths but needs to have a board edging to keep it from moving into the soil. Coloured gravel makes an attractive alternative to traditional grey.

The container enthusiast will see every box, pot, tin, basket or plastic bucket as a potential vegetable-holding possibility. The variety of containers is vast, ranging from traditional terracotta and recycled household items to modern galvanized iron.

growing

3

in containers

MOVABLE FEASTS
Aesthetics
Weight considerations
What to choose
Planting up a container
Growing potatoes in a barrel

WINDOW BOXES, GROW-BAGS AND HANGING BASKETS
Window boxes
Grow-bags
Planting a hanging basket
Support for grow-bags
Watering tips

◁ Metal containers provide a modern look for a combination of colourful tomatoes and bright red nasturtiums.

MOVABLE feasts

By using containers, you can move plants that are at their best to the forefront of the plantings, and when you have harvested them, they can be replaced with new stars.

- AESTHETICS

- WEIGHT CONSIDERATIONS

- WHAT TO CHOOSE
  Terracotta
  Galvanized iron
  Recycled containers

- PLANTING UP A CONTAINER

- GROWING POTATOES IN A BARREL

AESTHETICS

Containers are an essential element in the small-space vegetable grower's repertoire. On patios and balconies they are often the only available growing sites, and on the ground they offer focal points and provide height, for what is an essentially low-growing palette of plants. Arranging the containers can be as much part of the artistry of the vegetable garden as are the decisions as to which vegetables and varieties to grow for the maximum ornamental and productive value.

Growing plants in containers is labour-intensive and not the cheapest way of producing vegetables since you have to supply all the plant's needs, and you have to be on hand to water and feed on a regular basis. Plants growing in the ground can get their water and nutrients through their roots from what is available in the soil, but for container-grown plants, what you give them is all they get. However, in small spaces where you are close to the plants, it is easy to spot pests and diseases at an earlier stage and, if possible, to remedy the situation. One advantage is that you can be completely assured of organic produce.

WEIGHT CONSIDERATIONS

When planted up, some containers will be too large to be moved around and should be used as permanent growing sites. The weight of containers once filled with the plant and compost, and especially when watered, is a consideration that

△ Terracotta 'pouch' pots are among the most popular containers for vegetables and herbs. Provided it is relatively deep, it is possible to grow several different plants, such as parsley, in the pouches and a taller plant such as aubergine in the top of the pot.

needs to be accounted for early on in the planning of a roof garden or balcony. If you have any doubts about the weight that your roof can support, you may have to reconsider your vegetable empire and satisfy your desires by growing just a few salads and other vegetables in smaller containers and ringing the changes, when each container has been harvested. This can require a lot of forward planning as there always have to be several pots waiting in the wings.

◁ A child's wooden wheelbarrow has a second lease of life as a container for a number of pots of herbs. Line the base with plastic to protect it from water or place a plastic container in its base as a reservoir.

△ Galvanized metal containers are a recent stylish addition to the repertoire of plant containers. Site larger containers before you fill them with compost, or they will be too heavy to move later.

WHAT TO CHOOSE
Containers come in all materials, sizes and shapes, so it is possible to use them for artistic effects as well as productive sites for vegetables. Some are even fitted with castors so they can be moved around easily, even when planted.

and sizes, from flowerpots to large troughs. Special pots, such as strawberry pots, can be used for other plants, such as parsley and thyme.

• **Galvanized iron** containers bring a modern look to the vegetable garden and come in a range of shapes and sizes. If they don't come with drainage holes, either drill some across the base or add a good layer of drainage materials to the container before adding soil (see below).

• **Recycled containers** For a more quirky look, recycle large, brightly coloured olive cans or plant up a row of plastic buckets in jazzy colours. Old-fashioned butler's sinks make good containers but they are heavy. Even elegantly weathered stone urns can be pressed into service.

PLANTING UP A CONTAINER

The minimum size of pot for growing individual vegetables is a 25 cm (10 in) pot where there is a depth of soil not less than 20 cm (8 in). Most pots have drainage holes but some will need to have holes drilled in their bases.

1 First, put in place a drainage layer so that the plants are not growing in waterlogged soil. Gravel or a layer of old terracotta pot shards are the most suitable materials or you can use crumbled pieces of polystyrene packaging. Place a large piece of pot shard or other drainage materials over the drainage holes to prevent compost washing out each time you water the containers.

△ Small containers are ideal for herbs destined for a quick or short-term use. For a uniform look, apply a coat of white paint to terracotta and plastic pots.

• **Terracotta**, provided it is guaranteed to be frost-proof, is always attractive. On rooftops and balconies where weight is a consideration, plastic terracotta look-alikes are the more sensible.

Traditional terracotta offers warm colours, which provide a good decorative background for vegetables. It comes in a wide range of shapes

▷ Deep, old-fashioned ceramic sinks make useful, small-space containers for cut-and-come-again lettuce mixes.

△ Deep and colourful, former vegetable oil drums are cleaned and recycled to provide ample space for a variety of vegetables and herbs.

2 Fill the container with a lightweight, soilless compost, adding water-retaining gel or granules.
3 If the plant is tall and will need support, add canes or trellis, depending on the size of container and the type of plants, at the time of planting, rather than later in the plant's development to prevent damaging roots.
4 Water the compost well and allow it to settle before adding more, if necessary.
5 Make planting holes large enough to take the rootball of the plants, water them in well and firm them in, taking care not to damage the roots.

Water container-grown vegetables and fruit every day, and more frequently during dry, hot conditions. Avoid splashing water onto the leaves or flushing compost from the surface of the planting. If possible, place pots on plant saucers to hold surplus water as a reservoir for the plants and to avoid spillage and waste.

GROWING POTATOES IN A BARREL

In a small garden, try growing potatoes in a barrel or rubbish bin. Drill holes in the base and add pot shards and gravel for drainage.

1 Add a layer of garden compost and loam-based compost about 10 cm (4 in) deep.

2 Place four or five seed potatoes on top, then add another layer of soil. In a few weeks shoots will appear.

3 Once these shoots are 15–20 cm (6–8 in) tall, add more soil so that just their tips show. Water well and continue to cover the growing shoots each time they reach 15 cm (6 in) above the soil.

4 Once the soil has reached the top of the bin allow the shoots to grow. Harvest the potatoes after flowering.

WINDOW BOXES, GROW-BAGS
and hanging baskets

Even if you have no actual garden, you can still grow fresh herbs and vegetables in baskets, boxes and grow-bags, even if the range and quantity will be limited. These containers can be drafted in to grow your particular must-have fresh food choices, such as basil, tumbling trusses of cherry tomatoes, peppers, thyme and strawberries.

- WINDOW BOXES
- GROW-BAGS
- PLANTING A HANGING BASKET
- SUPPORT FOR GROW-BAGS
- WATERING TIPS

WINDOW BOXES

Space is restricted in these shallow containers but they will suit salad crops such as radishes and lettuces, which have shallow roots. Many herbs, such as chives, marjoram, parsley, thyme and sage, will also grow well in window boxes. Plant them towards the front of the box and set small tomatoes and peppers at the back of the box. Brighten the whole effect with nasturtiums which will also provide spicy leaves and flowers for your salads.

GROW-BAGS

Grow-bags may not be the most stylish of containers but they are extremely useful for large vegetables that crop over a long period, such as

tomatoes, peppers, courgettes, cucumbers, lettuces and aubergines. They consist of watertight plastic bags, filled with a peat or non-peat compost with added fertilizer.

To plant them up, you need to cut out sections of the plastic on the top of the bag to make a series of holes. Then set the plants into the compost through the holes. It is best to position grow-bags on a level surface, such as a patio, against a sunny wall in a sheltered site. Keep the compost moist because if it is allowed to dry out it will be difficult to re-wet.

Plants such as tomatoes and peppers will need a support system. There are several available commercially, and you can also make your own support systems using canes (see page 50).

△ Tomato 'Tumbler' produces prolific trusses of luscious, deep red cherry-type tomatoes on stems that trail over the edge of containers such as hanging baskets and windowboxes.

PLANTING A HANGING BASKET

Before you plant up the basket, check that the site that you have in mind for it is sufficiently strong and attach secure brackets that will support the quite considerable weight of plants and soil. Ensure the basket won't overhang the balcony, as dripping water from baskets will be annoying to neighbours below. Also make sure it isn't in a position where it will be inconvenient for you to reach or where you will constantly be hitting your head on it!

1 Stand the basket on a large upturned pot and line the inside of the basket with a home-made liner made from black plastic. Alternatively, use one of the many commercially available basket liners made from pressed peat or reconstituted wool shoddy.

2 Mix some compost with water-retaining gel crystals and add to the basket in layers. As you go, make small holes in the basket lining to push seedlings through, to give the planting a full and layered effect.

3 Gradually fill and plant up the sides of the basket until you put in place the plants in the top. Top up with compost, firm lightly and water well.

△ Runner beans in hanging baskets will not grow to the same height as those in the ground, but will nonetheless produce a reasonable crop of fresh beans.

◁ A terracotta window box is suitable for relatively low-growing herbs such as parsley, chervil and dill. Either plant the herbs directly into the container or use it as a 'cache-pot' to conceal individual pots.

SUPPORT FOR GROW-BAGS

If you are growing tomatoes in grow-bags they will need to be supported as they grow, especially when they have heavy trusses of fruit. It is simple to make your own supports using bamboo canes. As the plants grow, tie stems and trusses to the canes and wires.

1 Place the grow-bag on the ground. Push a cane through each of the rectangles cut in the plastic into the ground.

2 Strengthen with wire or string wound round canes and running between each one.

△ If a window box overhangs a balcony or juts out from a window it must be firmly fixed to railings or masonry. This wooden planter provides a lightweight cover for an inner plastic container.

▷ Site the hanging basket in a sunny position, sheltered from winds. Make sure that the bracket is securely fixed and that the basket is accessible for you to water and for harvesting.

WATERING TIPS

Regular watering of windowboxes, grow-bags and hanging baskets is crucial for the survival of the plants. Take care not to splash the foliage of plants. Watering hanging baskets requires extra care to avoid flushing out compost and exposing the roots. If possible, use a hanging basket with a hoist so you can lower it when you provide water to see where the water is flowing and control the amount. Alternatively, use a ladder or stand on a kitchen stool, so the basket is at eye-level or you are above it to see where the water flows.

Growing your own vegetables is one of gardening's most rewarding aspects. In limited spaces it is best to grow the vegetables that you enjoy most. Try out new varieties but give room to those that offer the bonus of colourful leaves, flowers and luscious harvests.

growing
vegetables

4

CHOOSING VEGETABLE VARIETIES
    Leaf vegetables
    Flower and fruiting vegetables
    Gourds
    Onion family
    Pods and kernels
    Roots, stems and bulbs
    Herbs and flowers

◁ Courgette plants do well in moist, fertile soils but can also be grown successfully in containers. Feed them well for a bumper crop.

CHOOSING
vegetable varieties

In a garden where space is limited, you need to choose the varieties carefully, opting for ones with compact growing habits, attractive foliage and plentiful crops.

- LEAF VEGETABLES
- FLOWER AND FRUITING VEGETABLES
- GOURDS
- ONION FAMILY
- PODS AND KERNELS
- ROOTS, STEMS AND BULBS
- HERBS AND FLOWERS

In a garden where space is limited, vegetables that take up large areas of the plot are on the transfer list. Cabbages, cauliflowers and Brussels sprouts belong to a group of vegetables known collectively as brassicas and are on my list of vegetables to avoid in small-space growing. They take up so much room with their large leaves and are hungry feeders. In my opinion, although fresh is best, there are other vegetables that have priority over them. Nonetheless, there are one or two brassicas that I will recommend as being suitable for the city kitchen garden, mainly because their ornamental qualities outweigh the disadvantages of their size (see Leaf vegetables and Flower and Fruiting vegetables, pages 55-57 and 58-59).

△ Brassicas are space- and nutrient-hungry plants. However, this attractive, dark-leaved kale, 'Nero di Toscano' grows well in containers and looks good in mixed borders.

◁ Lettuces, available in such a variety of leaf shapes and colours, are a priority for salad enthusiasts. Similarly, fresh carrots that you can eat raw or cooked are worth the space.

LEAF vegetables

LETTUCE

High on my list of preferences for the small garden are salads and to satisfy my love of variety in salads there is a wide choice of lettuces as well as of salad leaf collections.

Lettuce *(Lactuca sativa)*, the staple of most green salads, is the dominant leaf in these salad selections, but it comes in a range of leaf sizes, shapes, textures, colours and crunch. Lettuces are divided into different types according to the shape of their head and by season. The groups are butterhead, crisphead and iceberg, cos types and over-wintering lettuces. There is also a group of lettuces known as loose leaf, cut-and-come-again, and these special types are the basis for many of the salad selections available.

Many of the small lettuces such as 'Buttercrunch', 'Tom Thumb' and 'Little Gem' have very small compact heads and are ideal for windowboxes and other containers. They can be very closely planted (15–20 cm/6–8 in apart) and will still provide tasty, leafy produce. You can sow lettuce direct into cells or modules or direct into the growing site. In rows they should be 30 cm (12 in) apart with the seeds sown to a depth of 1 cm (½ in). They need regular watering once the seedlings are established, particularly in the week before harvesting. Butterheads take ten weeks to harvest, crisphead and cos types are ready at 14 weeks.

Choices: For red or mahogany-bronze leaves that look attractive in the garden

△ Lettuce 'Little Gem'.

and in salads try 'Little Leprechaun', 'Lollo Rosso', 'Marvel of Four Seasons' or 'Red Salad Bowl'. Greenest of green leaves come from 'Lollo Biondo', while 'Salad Bowl' with fresh green, heavily indented leaves is a cut-and-come-again type. Choose 'Buttercrunch', 'Tom Thumb' and 'Little Gem' for compact container growth.

SALAD ROCKET

Salad rocket *(Eruca sativa)* is one of the hottest of the salad leaves, offering attractive indented green leaves and white flowers, which are equally hot to taste. Wild rocket has long, deeply-cut leaves and is useful as a cut-and-come-again crop. Providing similar ferocity in a relatively small leaf is American landcress *(Barbarea montana)*, which has bright yellow flowers.

SALAD LEAF COLLECTIONS

These salads with foliage of differing colour, texture and taste are relatively expensive to buy from supermarkets, but can be grown and picked fresh over a long period in the year.

Among the seed selections are international salad collection packs such as English, Italian, American, French and Oriental. These combine salads that are typical for each type of cuisine and will make colourful container selections as well as look good in the ground. All have some leaves which are spicy and others which have a good background, almost bland flavour. In addition the leaves have different textures, colours and shapes, making an attractive small clump in the garden or in a container. The oriental mixture of seeds is a particularly good choice because they are extremely versatile. They can be sown in mid to late summer and used more or less as cut-and-come-again crops, or allowed to grow to full size and used as individual vegetables. They can also be over-wintered under cloches.

A French collection is likely to include herbs such as chervil, as well as leaves of lamb's lettuce or corn salad, chicory and lettuce. An Italian collection might contain salad rocket, chicory, radicchio and lettuce 'Lollo Rosso' together with the herb basil, while an Oriental collection will include a wide range of over-wintering plants such as Pak Choi, purple mustard, mizuna and mibuna.

△ Oriental salad greens.

'Oriental vegetables' is the collective name given to a range of mainly cabbages or brassicas which can be grown as cut-and-come-again crops or as individual rows of single-type seed packs. They include Chinese cabbage, oriental mustard, mustard spinach (Komatsuna), Pak Choi, Japanese greens (mizuna) and Japanese parsley (mitsuba). They are often sold in a mixed pack called Oriental Saladini. They grow well in sun in fertile soil and need to be well-watered. If grown as a cut-and-come-again crop you can start to pick leaves about four weeks after sowing, taking just enough to keep the plants producing more leaves for later harvests. If growing in rows as individual vegetable plants, allow 30 cm (12 in) between the rows.

CHICORY

Chicory *(Cichorium intybus)* is available as forcing chicory and as leaf chicory. Forcing chicory is blanched to a fresh spring green colour and has closely packed, upright leaves and a slightly bitter taste. Leaf chicory can be harvested as individual leaves or allowed to form a heart and harvested whole. It comes in many attractive colourings, including red. Red chicory or radicchio adds marbled colouring to salads and looks particularly attractive in the winter vegetable garden and salad bowl. Green leaf form or sugarloaf chicory has large lettuce-like heads and is a good over-wintering salad leaf. Chicory grows well in fertile, well-drained soil.

Sow forcing chicory in late spring or early summer direct into rows in the

ground and thin to 20 cm (8 in) when the first true leaves begin to appear. Water well throughout the season. In autumn dig the plants up, harvest the foliage for use in salads, cutting them back so that about 2 cm (¾ in) of foliage is showing above the root. Cut back the roots and plant up several to a pot in moist compost. Place a second pot upside down on the rim of the first pot to act as a cover, and leave in a frost-free site for up to 12 weeks. Once the new tips are growing well they can be harvested.

Sow leaf chicory into seed trays in spring and plant out in early summer. It will be ready to harvest in summer, but you can also sow in midsummer for an autumn harvest and in late summer for growing under a cloche in winter.
Choices: Forcing chicory: 'Brussels Witloof', 'Zoom'. Leaf forms: 'Sugar Loaf', 'Palla Rossa', 'Rossa de Treviso', 'Variegata de Sottamarina'.

CURLY KALE

Curly kale *(Brassica oleracea* Acephala Group) is an appetizing winter vegetable if you pick its leaves when they are young and tender. It is one of the vegetables I consider too space-hungry for the small garden. However, there are two forms that I grow because of their wonderfully ornamental foliage. They do taste good, too, but need to be harvested when the leaves are young, which defeats my ornamental objectives somewhat!

You will need a seedling nursery bed, or container if you are growing on a balcony or patio, to hold the young plants until they are ready to plant out in late summer into their growing sites. Sow seed direct into the seed bed or a container in early spring and thin the seedlings as they mature. Water well. They are tall-growing and, if combining vegetables and flowers in a border, will suit the middle of the border. They will need supporting as the foliage rosette becomes heavy and in windy conditions may overbalance.

Choices: 'Darkibor' has deeply curled green leaves, while 'Red Bor' has similarly deeply-cut but purple-bronze leaves. 'Nero di Toscana' has an embossed, bubble-like texture to its foliage which is such a dark green that it is almost black. 'Dwarf Curled' is good for the small-space garden.

CHARD

Once just available in its greenleaf form, with a striking white stem, chard *(Beta vulgaris* Cicla Group) is now available in a mixture of stem and leaf colours, adding emphasis to its ornamental qualities in the vegetable garden and in combination with flowering plants. Grow it in nitrogen-rich, fertile soil and add bulky organic matter or material from your compost bin. Sow in late spring through to midsummer for harvest during the following winter and late spring. Chard needs space so thin seedlings to 30 cm (12 in) apart. The plants need water and liquid fertilizing when young. They can be grown more closely together but this will cramp the plants and reduce the leaf size. Chard stems and leaves are cooked separately, as the leaves need a shorter

▷ Chard 'Bright Lights'.

cooking time than the stems, which can be used as an asparagus substitute.

Choices: 'Burgundy Chard' has reddish stems and attractively veined leaves, 'Rhubarb Chard' has similarly deep red stems and veining. 'Bright Lights' is a seed mixture containing chard with stems in a range of shades including red, white, pink, green and yellow. The foliage is also attractive with a bronze shiny texture and strong veining. The leaves are ready 60 days from sowing. 'Lucullus' has plain white stems and white veining on the smooth foliage.

LAMB'S LETTUCE

Lamb's lettuce *(Valerianella locusta),* also known as corn salad, is a hardy annual with a dark green bitter-tasting leaf that makes a useful addition to a winter salad. It grows well in full sun or shade in fertile, moist but not water-logged soils. Sow in spring in rows and thin to 10–15 cm (4–6 in) apart, water well and sow successionally throughout the summer for later crops. Late sowings can be successfully over-wintered under cloches.

Choices: 'Verte de Cambrai', 'Vit'.

FLOWER and FRUITING vegetables

TOMATOES

Tomatoes (*Lycopersicon esculentum*) are among the sunniest fruits of the vegetable garden. Plum, beefsteak, cherry, striped, yellow, orange, red and even bronze-black are the shapes and colours available. Many seed companies have ranges of old or heritage seeds or young plants, which provide luscious fruits in even more exciting shapes and colours. With evocative names such as 'Broad Ripple Yellow Cream', 'Banana Legs' and 'Black Russian', they are frost-tender so grow them in a greenhouse, or plant outdoor varieties in the warmest site when all frost danger has passed.

There are two main types, described as bush or cordons, depending on their growth habits. Bush types need little attention, but cordons need to have side shoots taken out regularly so the plants concentrate their energies on producing a limited number of well-formed, good quality fruiting branches (trusses). When cordons have set fruit on at least 3–4 trusses, pinch out the main growing tip. If you have a wall for them to shelter against and can grow them on canes or a firm support system, cordons will provide a good crop. Some bush types that have a sprawling habit grow well in containers, hanging baskets and windowboxes.

All tomatoes need full sun in a sheltered site in fertile, well-drained soil. Sow seed onto the surface of a seed tray or into a modular tray, and just cover with a little compost. Enclose the tray in a polythene bag and either place in a propagator or site where the temperature is 15–18°C (60–65°F). Prick the seedlings out when the first true leaves appear and as weather warms in early summer harden off plants during the day before planting out into the garden, or taking pots out onto a roof garden or patio. If you are growing in containers and especially in grow-bags, water regularly.

Container choices: 'Tumbler' is a popular choice for containers of all kinds and produces abundant small red fruits.

'Tornado' has abundant small red cherry-sized fruits, while 'Sun Belle' has small yellow, mini-plum shaped fruits. 'Tiny Tim' is ideal for window-boxes and produces good red fruits. 'Tornado' suits containers and hanging baskets. For growing in the ground choose 'Golden Sunrise', 'San Marzano' (a plum tomato), 'Gardeners' Delight' (large trusses of small well-flavoured fruits) and 'Sweet Cherry' (masses of small red fruits).

▽ Tomato 'Tumbler'.

PEPPERS

Peppers *(Capsicum annuum)*, often called sweet bell or wax peppers, with brightly coloured bell-shaped fruits in yellow, green, red and purple, need greenhouse protection in cold temperate climates, but can be planted out into the sunniest, most sheltered position in the garden or patio in summer. Sow two seeds per pot or cell, if using modular seed trays, in early spring and provide a temperature of 21°C (70°F). As the seedlings germinate and establish, reduce the heat to 12–15°C (55–60°F). Transplant them when their first flowers appear and, after hardening off, grow in grow-bags or other containers. Provide liquid fertilizer and water the plants well if in containers. The fruits are ready to harvest when green, but if you leave them on the plants they will ripen over a three week period to red, yellow or purple depending on variety.

Choices: 'Big Banana' has long red fruits, 'Sweet Chocolate' has dark, almost black-skinned fruit. Mixed selections of yellow, orange, green, red and black peppers are also available.

AUBERGINE

The aubergine *(Solanum melongena)* needs high heat over a long period in summer if it is to fruit outdoors, otherwise it needs to be grown in a greenhouse. The most familiar deep purple, glossy skinned fruits are preceded by attractive mauve flowers if the temperature is at a constant 25–30°C (75–86°F). Also available is a range of unusually shaped and coloured aubergines, varying from white tennis-ball-sized fruits to long, thin, marbled-skinned ones.

△ Peppers 'Banana Supreme'.

Sow seed in spring into trays in a propagator where you can achieve a temperature of 15–21°C (58–70°F). Pot on when the seedlings are large enough to handle and harden off before planting outside. They need to be in full sun in a sheltered site in a well-drained, fertile soil. If growing in containers and grow-bags, keep the plants well watered and use a liquid fertilizer. Stake the plants with cane supports.

When the flowers bloom spray with a fine water mister to increase pollination and nip off side shoots when up to six fruits have formed on the plant. Harvest fruits in late summer.

Choices: 'Mini Bambino' is a short plant that produces mini-aubergines that can be cooked and served whole. 'Long Purple' and 'Black Enorma' produce large fruits. 'Red Egg' is a new offering with bright red fruits that grows well in containers. 'Chinese Ancestors' is a new collection of aubergines in different shapes and colours, including white, purple and green, in long, round and standard shapes. 'Mr Stripey' has a marbled white and purple skin, while 'Kermit' is a new white-skinned, apple-shaped aubergine. 'Bonica' produces early fruits.

SPROUTING BROCCOLI

Sprouting broccoli *(Brassica oleracea Italica Group)* is another of the space-hungry brassicas that I like to give garden room to because they are attractive and good value in terms of taste and timing. There are two forms, both with green leaves but having purple or green flowers, which are the sprouting shoots that are harvested.

You will need a space to house the seedlings over the spring and early summer until transplanting to their final growing positions. Sow seeds into rows in a seedbed and thin to 15 cm (6 in) apart. Transplant to the final growing site in midsummer with 68–75 cm (27–30 in) between plants and between rows. Sprouting broccoli needs a sunny position in deep, free-draining but moist soil. Water well and regularly.

Sprouting broccoli will provide a regular harvest through the late winter and into early spring. Plants may need staking or earthing up at the roots to provide extra stability. Remove the central shoot and pick the prolific purple or green flowering shoots as they appear. Keep cutting to ensure regular shoot production.

Choices: 'Early Purple Sprouting' is ready in late winter; 'Early White Sprouting' in early spring. Choose 'Red Arrow' for purple spears over a long period.

GOURDS

Within this group of large fruits are many of my favourite vegetables including courgettes (immature marrows), squash and pumpkins. While courgettes, pumpkins and squash are the fruits of large space-demanding, sprawling plants, I include them in the small urban garden because they are rewarding in terms of ornament and use, as well as nutrition and kitchen variety. And as they have a vining, climbing habit you can grow them in a more limited space than you might at first think possible.

COURGETTE

Courgette *(Cucurbita pepo)* or zucchini are the immature fruits of the marrow and grow well in fertile, moist soils. If grown in containers provide them with regular and copious amounts of water as they are thirsty plants. Their flowers are also edible and look attractive served with mini-courgettes attached. Pick the courgettes regularly when they are about 10–15 cm (4–6 in) long. If you leave them on the plant the crop numbers will reduce and individual fruits will be large and marrow-like.

Either sow seed in early spring in a heated propagator or two or three seeds directly into the ground once all frost danger is over. If direct sowing into the ground cover the sowing site with a mini-cloche, such as a plastic bottle with its bottom removed. This will act as a mini-greenhouse and warm the soil around the germinating seedling. When the seedlings have germinated, thin them to leave just one seedling.

△ Courgette 'Gold Rush'.

Choices: 'Black Forest' is a climbing variety that is useful for covering trellis and arches and for small-space growing. 'Ambassador' is also a compact plant and for a colourful crop outdoors and in the kitchen, 'Jemmer', 'Gold Rush' and 'Taxi' are yellow-skinned courgettes.

PUMPKIN AND SQUASH

Pumpkin *(Cucurbita maxima)* and squash *(Cucurbita moschata)* are annual vining plants that will rush along the ground or rise, like jungle creatures, up supports to reach the sunshine. If you do grow them over supports make sure they are strong as these fruits and foliage are very weighty. Most pumpkins are too large for the small garden but there are several that produce prolific small fruits that provide meals in

themselves and can be very decorative in the vegetable garden. Squash are nutty textured and come in all shapes and sizes. Like pumpkin, they keep well over the winter if cured in the sun after harvest and stored in a dry frost-free site until ready for use. Sowing is as for courgettes. In containers they need to be well watered at the base of the plant.

Choices: 'Jack be Little' and 'Baby Bear' are small pumpkins, the former just fitting into the palm of your hand. 'Crown Prince' with a bluish skin is a very densely textured pumpkin, which is perfect for savoury dishes; it also looks attractive in the garden.

In the squash family there are many small and attractive fruits including 'Butternut', 'Kaboucha', 'Table Ace' and 'Sweet Dumpling'.

ONION family

LEEKS

Leeks *(Allium porrum)* are one of the staples of the autumn and winter kitchen garden, providing pungent onion flavour and attractive strappy foliage in grey and silvery tones. In addition, if your soil is heavy the leek's root system will help to improve soil structure. They do well in open sites in average garden soil. Sow seed directly into a seed bed in spring, 2.5 cm (1 in) deep and 15 cm (6 in) apart.

When the seedlings are about as thick as your little finger and 20 cm (8 in) tall, usually about 12 weeks after sowing, transplant them into their growing site. Before lifting, water them well and make planting holes 15–20 cm (6–8 in) deep and 15 cm (6 in) apart. Use a trowel to lift the young plants, and trim the leaves a little and drop them into individual planting holes. Swirl water into the planting hole but don't back fill with soil. Keep the row weed-free and water regularly. Harvest by lifting the plants with a fork.

Choices: 'Carentan' and 'Natan' produce sturdy white stems and have attractive grey-green foliage. 'King Richard' has a long white shaft and is a good choice for growing at a closer spacing to produce mini-leeks. 'Musselburgh' is a popular old variety.

ONIONS

Onions *(Allium cepa)* are grown for their tasty swollen bulbs and can be raised from specially prepared small onions called onion sets, or from seed. If you

△ Leeks 'King Richard'.

are growing vegetables in a small space and don't have a greenhouse or room for a seedbed, then the solution is to grow onions from sets.

There are two disadvantages to growing from sets. You may not have the same range of varieties available as sets as there are seeds. Onions grown from sets tend to run to flower or 'bolt', so buy sets that are labelled as 'heat-treated'. Sets are available from seed merchants and garden centres.

Onions need well-drained, fertile soil in a sunny open site. Plant sets into the ground in autumn or from late winter right the way through to mid-spring, in rows, just covering them with soil so that the tips just show above the soil surface. They should be 5 cm (2 in) apart. If you have the space and facilities to grow from seed, sow indoors in

winter and provide temperatures of 10–16°C (50–60°F). After hardening off the seedlings, plant them out into their growing site in spring. Spring, salad or bunching onions can be sown in succession through the growing season in spring and summer. They can be sown direct into the ground and thinned to 2.5 cm (1 in).

Choices: 'Ailsa Craig' produces mild-flavoured bulbs, but is not a good keeping onion. 'Autumn Gold' is a good keeper. 'New Fen Globe' is available in heat-treated sets. For attractive colour and strong flavour, the red onion 'Red Baron' is a good keeping onion. 'White Lisbon' and 'White Lisbon Winter Hardy' are two bunching onions that will give you salad material right throughout the year.

△ Onion 'Ailsa Craig'.

PODS and KERNELS

BEANS

There are several species of bean that provide ornamental flowers, well-coloured tasty pods or beans that will suit small spaces and containers. Runner beans and some French or haricot beans are climbing plants that will provide good cover on trellises or can be used as screens on patios.

Runner beans

Runner beans (*Phaseolus coccineus*) will do best in sites that have been well-prepared in the autumn and winter before planting in spring. They grow best in a warm sheltered site with a little shade. They are frost tender so should either be sown indoors and transplanted when all frost danger is past, or sown direct into the growing site in late spring or early summer when the soil temperature has risen to about 10°C (50°F).

Runner beans need supporting and the traditional way to do this is with canes and twine. Either make a circular wigwam of canes, tied at the top like a teepee, or have a double row of canes tied to each other at the top, and linked along the whole row by canes laid across the V-shaped tops of the cane rows. You can also set the canes into the ground as uprights and secure bean or pea netting to them or use twine to give the beans a foothold.

Pinch out the tops of the bean plants when they reach the top of the canes. Water well and regularly, particularly when in flower. Sometimes a fine spray on the flowers aids pollination if bees are

in short supply or the flowers are infested with pollen beetles, which deter bees. Harvest regularly from mid-summer to keep pod production going.
Choices: 'Flamenco' and 'Relay' have flowers in three colours – white, red and bi-colour – and 'Flamenco' is a low-growing compact plant that will suit containers. 'White Lady' has plain white flowers and produces long, smooth, stringless pods. 'Painted Lady' is an old variety with white and red bi-coloured flowers and well-flavoured pods. 'Prize winner', 'Lady Di' and 'Galaxy' are among the red-flowered varieties. 'Hestia' is a dwarf runner bean with a good flavour, producing long, straight, stringless pods. It has bi-coloured flowers and, like all runner beans, is attractive in containers and in the small vegetable garden.

△ French bean 'Barlotta Lingua di Fuoco'.

French beans

French beans (*Phaseolus vulgaris*), also known as dwarf and snap beans, are usually small and bushy although there are some climbing varieties. Their pods are green, purple or yellow. They are frost tender so should either be started early indoors and transplanted outside when all danger of frost has past or sown direct outside when soil temperature is around 13°C (56°F). From late spring through to midsummer you can sow outdoors to provide a successional crop. Sow seeds 3 cm (1 in) deep in soil and leave 23 cm (9 in) between plants. They grow best in full sun in a fertile, slightly acid soil in a sheltered position and need regular watering, particularly when in flower.
Choices: Climbing forms include 'Barlotta Lingua di Fuoco' which has attractively pink-and-cream marbled skins on pods and on the beans, which can be used as haricots towards the end of the growing season. 'Corona d'Oro' is a yellow podded climber, 'Cosse Violette' has purple pods and 'Kentucky Blue' produces long pods ready to pick 8–9 weeks after sowing. The ultimate in colour and taste comes from the lablab or hyacinth bean (*Dolichos lablab*) 'Ruby Moon', which has flat purple pods and flowers.

For bush or dwarf beans, 'Sungold' is a golden yellow pod on a compact bushy plant, 'Royalty' and 'Purple Tepee' are purple-podded bush beans, while 'Aramis' and 'Maxi' are prolific green-podded bush beans.

Broad beans

Broad beans (*Vicia faba*) are very hardy and can be sown in late autumn/early winter to over-winter and crop from early summer. They grow well in heavy but not water-logged soil in sun. Sow in double rows 20 cm (8 in) apart. A system of posts with string attached will keep plants upright and stop them being toppled in windy conditions. They can also be sown in late winter to provide a crop in summer. Pinch out the growing tips once the first flowers have set.

Choices: 'Aquadulce' is an old variety that crops well from early winter sowing. 'Green Windsor' has short pods with fewer beans but is well-flavoured. 'Red Epicure' has startling red beans inside the green pod. 'The Sutton' is a dwarf bush form with good yields. Broad beans have white flowers, but heritage seed with crimson flowers is available from specialist seed suppliers.

PEAS

Peas (*Pisum sativum*) are scrambling annuals in two forms – as shelling peas, which are taken out of the pods after harvest, and as pod or mangetout peas, where the whole pod and the immature peas within it are eaten. You can sow to over-winter for harvesting in late spring, but in a small space it is simpler to sow direct into the ground or containers in spring. They need well-watered, fertile, well-prepared soil and will tolerate some shade but need to be supported early on. A twiggy framework of hazel pea-sticks is useful once the peas are growing well, forming a decorative low hedge or screen. Holly

△ Pea 'Sugar Snap'.

leaves along the line of the sowing may put off mice and wire netting tunnels hooped over seedlings will deter birds.

Choices: Mangetout or snap peas: 'Sugar Snap', 'Oregon Sugar Pod' and 'Ambrosia' will provide tender and juicy pods over a long period.

Early garden or pod peas: 'Tafila' is one of the earliest to crop and has semi-leafless stems. 'Kelvedon Wonder', 'Early Onward' and 'Daybreak' are good prolific early peas, while for a maincrop choose 'Alderman'. 'Hurst Green Shaft' and 'Onward' produce pods packed with plump peas. For extra ornamental value, grow the pink-red flowered 'Yuhsaya'.

SWEETCORN

Sweetcorn (*Zea mays*) or corn on the cob provides sweet kernels in regimented rows along its length. Yellow or creamy-white are the usual colours, but there are also some colourful varieties.

Some are strictly ornamental while others have an excellent flavour as well.

Sweetcorn is a tall plant and as it is wind-pollinated it is best to grow it in blocks so plants can cross-pollinate. Although it needs wind for pollination, it should be grown in a relatively sheltered position. Earthing up the soil around the plant's roots will help keep it stable in unsheltered sites. Grow in full sun in a free-draining but moisture-retentive, fertile, slightly acid soil. It needs warmth to germinate and soil temperatures above 10°C (50°F).

Sow indoors, two to three seeds per pot, in late spring at a temperature of 13°C (55°F). Once the seedlings are growing remove all but the strongest one from the pot. Harden off and plant out when all frost danger is past. Plants need to be about 35 cm (14 in) apart, but can be more closely planted in containers. Water regularly, especially when in flower. Once the silks or tassels turn brown they are ready to harvest.

Choices: New varieties of sweetcorn, bred for their sweetness, are often described as Supersweet. If you grow them with older varieties, they are likely to cross-pollinate each other, resulting in a loss of sweetness in the newer varieties. It's therefore best to grow the different types quite separate from each other. 'Sweet Nugget' is a supersweet variety with a deep yellow, long cob. 'Sunrise' is a compact plant that can be closely planted. 'Honey and Cream' has white and yellow kernels on the cob but is tall growing. 'Blue Jade' produces small cobs with blue kernels; it has a dwarf, bushy shape and suits containers or small spaces.

ROOTS, STEMS and BULBS

POTATOES

Potatoes (*Solanum tuberosum*) may seem to be too space-hungry for the small garden, but the taste of home-grown potatoes outweighs that caveat. There are special varieties bred for close growing and methods of growing in containers which, although they won't yield an over-abundant crop, will produce enough for the small-space gardener to enjoy (see page 47). Seed merchants and garden centres are recognizing this fact and selling packs of smaller quantities of seed potatoes. There are also numerous old varieties sold described as heritage varieties which have been worked on to improve their disease- and pest-resistance. They offer good taste and in many cases well-coloured skins for salads as well as swirls of colour within the potato flesh itself.

If you have the space, grow varieties from the three main harvests: early potatoes (ready for harvest about 8–10 weeks after planting), second early (ready from mid to late summer), as well as a late or main crop potato. Potatoes are susceptible to many diseases so buy certified virus-free seed potatoes and choose varieties that are more dis-ease-resistant. Early crops are useful as they are harvested before slugs and wireworms can damage them.

Seed potatoes have to be prepared to make them shoot before planting out. Egg boxes make suitable containers to stand seed potatoes or tubers in. Keep the potatoes in a cool, frost-free and light site for about six weeks while they 'chit' or send out small shoots.

Plant the tubers into trenches in the well-drained, fertile soil in a sunny site. Early varieties go in from early to mid-spring, with main crops planted from mid- to late spring. Keep the tubers about 30 cm (12 in) apart and main crops 38 cm (15 in) apart with 50–75 cm (20–30 in) between rows, with early potatoes closer together than the main crop varieties. Protect the rows with a cover of horticultural fleece, especially if frosts are forecast.

When shoots appear above ground, fork up the soil in the rows to make a ridge above the potatoes to protect them from frosts and to keep them out of the light. If they have contact with light they will turn green and become poisonous. Water the soil around the plants well in dry weather.

Many varieties have attractive flowers and these are a useful indicator

△ Potato 'Foremost'.

of when to harvest. Early potatoes are ready to harvest when the flowers are opening on the stems (about 9–10 weeks from planting), while main crops are left in the ground until autumn when the flowering stems die down. Dig them up, allow to dry off and store in the dark in a cool, frost-free site. Early potatoes are thin-skinned and delicious eaten soon after harvest. They are not suitable for storing. Second earlies and main crop are larger and suitable for storing.

Choices: 'Dunluce' is an extra early potato with compact growth and suits forcing in pots in a greenhouse or in containers. 'Foremost' is a first early which also has compact growth and is usually left untouched by slugs. 'Kestrel' is a second early with good resistance to slugs. 'Valor' is a main crop potato which is compact and resistant to tuber blight with good tolerance of eelworm. 'Mimi' is a new cherry-sized, red-skinned punnet potato. It is lifted early and treated as an early crop, but can be planted closer than traditional early potatoes.

CARROTS

Carrots (*Daucus carrota*) can be sown in succession to provide harvests at different times during the year. Traditionally grown for their long, fat roots, there are also short-rooted vari-eties which are useful for container growing or for heavy soils. Carrots need full sun in a well-prepared site and plenty of water. Short-rooted varieties take only 15 weeks to mature, so even though you won't have the traditional carrot shape you will have several harvests of sweet and succulent stump-rooted carrots.

Sow seed at the beginning of spring into shallow rows 12 mm (½ in) deep and 15 cm (6 in) apart. Carrot seed is fine, and pelleted or coated seeds are easier to sow. Cover with soil and water well. Protect the row with a cloche if sowing early in spring until the plants are growing well. Carrot rootfly is a serious pest (see page 27).

Choices: 'Amsterdam Forcing' matures early. 'Redca' is suitable on shallow soils. 'Early Market' is a short-rooted carrot with good flavour and colour. 'Early Nantes' is a good carrot for the small garden and 'Parmex' and 'Parabell' are two varieties with almost round roots. 'Flyaway' is a good main crop, long-rooted carrot with resistance to carrot fly.

RADISHES

Radishes *(Raphanus sativus)*, grown for their spicy and colourful swollen roots, come in many shapes, sizes and colours. Salad radishes are fast-growing and ready to harvest four weeks after sowing; winter varieties take longer to mature. Radishes need a light, well-drained but moist and well-prepared soil. Summer-sown radishes need a little shade, so are useful for intercropping.

Sow small amounts of radish seed at regular intervals in short rows and thin to 2.5 cm (1 in) between plants. Winter radishes need up to 15 cm (6 in) between plants. They should be sown

△ Carrot 'Amsterdam Forcing'.

during summer for autumn and winter harvests, while salad radishes can be sown from early spring through to autumn.

Choices: 'Cherry Belle', 'French Breakfast' and 'Scarlet Globe' are good salad radishes, while 'China Rose', with white flesh, and 'Mantanghong', with crimson flesh, are good winter varieties.

BEETROOT

Beetroot *(Beta vulgaris)* provides young leaves that spice up salads in terms of colour and taste, as well as its swollen root which is delicious eaten as a hot vegetable or pickled for cold use. There are many shapes, ranging from round, globe shapes to long, thin tapering roots. New types described as 'monogerm' varieties can be sown more closely spaced as they don't need to be thinned and are ideal for small-space growing.

Beetroot needs a light, well-drained and well-prepared soil. Soak seeds for

up to an hour to reduce effects of the natural germination inhibitor they contain. Non-monogerm seed is a small beetroot fruit containing up to three seeds, so if all three germinate thin them eventually to a distance of 10 cm (4 in). Sow seed in mid-spring into rows, if necessary protecting with cloches to warm the soil up. Thin the seedlings, as necessary, and mulch the row to conserve water and to reduce weeds.

Choices: For baby beets and to avoid the task of thinning, use a monogerm variety such as 'Monogram', 'Moneta' and 'Monopoly'. Beetroot does have a reputation for bolting, so choose varieties described as bolt-resistant such as 'Bolthardy', 'Regala' (good for container growing) and 'Detroit 6 Rubidus'. For unusual coloured beets choose 'Burpee's Golden' with yellow flesh and 'Chioggia Pink' with rings of pink and white flesh, which fade on cooking. Best for baby beets are 'Tardel' and 'Detroit 2 Little Ball'.

△ Beetroot 'Bolthardy'.

KOHLRABI

Kohlrabi (*Brassica oleracea* Gongylodes Group) is a swollen stem which can be grated raw into salads or cooked and served whole or sliced. It is available in green and purple forms, making it an ornamental as well as a productive vegetable.

Kohlrabi needs a sunny site in a well-drained, fertile soil. It can be grown as a mini-vegetable and suits container growing well. It needs to be well-watered regularly otherwise the centre becomes woody. Apply a high-nitrogen fertilizer during the growing season and, if growing in containers, apply a general fertilizer every three weeks.

Sow into the ground in late winter but protect tender seedlings with cloches. Continue to sow through the spring and summer to keep a succession of plants going. You can also sow in autumn for a later harvest, but this sowing will need the protection of cloches. Harvest from midsummer onwards when the kohlrabi is well-rounded and about the size of a tennis ball.

Choices: 'Green Delicacy' and 'Purple Delicacy' offer green and purple skins and good leaf colourings as well.

PARSNIP

Parsnip (*Pastinaca sativa*) is a winter-hardy root vegetable which grows best in full sun in a light soil. If your soil is heavy or you are growing in containers, use one of the stump-rooted varieties. Sow seed direct into the growing site from late winter through to early spring. Parsnips should always be sown direct as they dislike root disturbance. Thin the seedlings out to about 15 cm (6 in)

△ Turnip 'Milan Purple Top'.

between plants. Water regularly and keep the site weed-free. Harvest parsnips from mid-autumn onwards through the winter.

Choices: Parsnips tend to get a disease called canker, so choose resistant varieties such as 'Avonresister' which also produces small roots, so is suited to small-space and container growing.

TURNIP

Turnip (*Brassica rapa*) is a fast-growing root vegetable that can be used raw in salads or cooked. It grows well in alkaline, well-drained soil in a sunny open site that was manured for the previous crop grown on the site. Sow direct outdoors in early spring and late summer, avoiding sowing in early or midsummer as hot weather induces turnips to bolt. Protect early sown seedlings with cloches if necessary. Thin first sowings to 12 cm (5 in) just as the seedlings establish and later sowings to 23 cm

(9 in). Check for flea beetles and water well in dry weather, keep weed-free and harvest early sowings from late spring into early summer and later or maincrop sowings from mid-autumn. You can leave them in the ground over winter, but they will need some protection. A mulch of straw is probably suitable.

Choices: 'Golden Ball' has yellow flesh and matures in about 60 days from a spring sowing. 'Milan Purple Top' is a flattened root which matures quickly and is good for early sowing. 'Veitch's Red Globe' has dark red skin and white flesh and is also suitable for an early sowing. Use its leaves as a spinach substitute. 'Green Top Stone' can be sown late in autumn for winter use.

BABY VEGETABLES

Close spacing some vegetable varieties results in mini-versions of the mature form, packed full of flavour and offering 'designer' vegetables on a small-scale. Also known as mini-vegetables or high density vegetables, many have been bred to perform well at closer spacing than traditional vegetables. They are high yielding, making them a perfect choice for small-space gardening. Cabbages and cauliflowers produce mini-heads if grown to a spacing of 10 cm (4 in) and 15 cm (6 in) respectively, while leeks will be pencil-thin and just as tasty as full-size leeks if spaced to 1 cm (½ in). In some cases you will need to check seed catalogues to see which varieties are recommended for growing as baby vegetables.

HERBS and FLOWERS

Culinary herbs such as thyme *(Thymus spp.)*, rosemary *(Rosmarinus officinalis)*, parsley *(Petroselinum crispum)*, sage *(Salvia officinalis)*, summer savory *(Satureja montana)*, bay *(Laurus nobilis)*, chives *(Allium schoenoprasum)*, mint *(Mentha* spp.*)* and basil *(Occimum basilicum)* are among the popular choices for kitchen gardens.

Herbs can be grown in straight rows in the garden or mixed in with the flower border and many of them grow well in containers. Rosemary and bay can be grown into standard shapes and used as formal ornamental features as well as for the kitchen. Thyme in its creeping forms suits hanging baskets and both ordinary chives and garlic chives have flowers that are pretty enough to fit into the flower border. Sage comes in a range of leaf colours and combines well with perennials. It also makes a good container plant.

Mint, one of the natural thugs of the herb garden, spreading quickly by its vigorous root-runners, is a perfect herb to grow in containers. There are several variegated forms, including striped golden and green ginger mint, which will offer ornamental value. Mint can be cut back after flowering and one or two roots potted up and brought indoors to continue growing over the winter.

Many herbs are available from supermarkets already potted up, so if you don't have space to grow your own, buy them on a regular basis and pot them on and grow them for the short term on the patio or balcony, using them as you need them.

△ The flowers of the pot marigold are edible.

EDIBLE FLOWERS

Many herb flowers, including chives, summer savory, rosemary and basil, have wonderfully aromatic flavours and can be added to salads. Other flowers such as nasturtium *(Tropaeoleum majus)*, heartsease *(Viola tricolor)* and pot marigold *(Calendula officinalis)* provide colour and flavour to food. There are many garden flowers whose petals can be eaten, but unless you are sure that a plant is edible, do not eat it!

Pick the flowers early in the day and rinse them under a cold tap to dislodge any lurking insects. Dry them on absorbent paper towels and keep in the refrigerator in plastic boxes until you are ready to use them.

△ Herbs look attractive grown between the spokes of a cartwheel raised up on bricks.

In a city kitchen garden, a generous orchard with numerous trees is not possible, but with planning you can maximize your harvest of luscious soft fruits and juicy top fruits. Home-grown fruit has the edge in terms of satisfaction and unbeatable flavour.

fruit

5

CHOOSING FRUIT VARIETIES
The right rootstock, Special shapes

CHOOSING FRUIT TREES
Avoiding problems, Pollinators for apples
Planting fruit trees, Awaiting fruit

GROWING SOFT FRUIT
Choosing varieties, Practicalities

GROWING STRAWBERRIES
The plants, Making space
Planting, Table-top system

SHRUBBY FRUITS
Gooseberies, Redcurrants, Blackcurrants
Blueberries, Frost protection

GROWING CANE FRUITS
Raspberries, Blackberries
Hybrid berries

◁ This shady arbour is framed by a grapevine growing on a pergola.
Cane fruit, such as raspberries, and ornamental plants surround it.

CHOOSING fruit varieties

Soft fruit, such as strawberries, raspberries and blackberries, and top fruit, including apples, pears and peaches, can be grown in the ground as well as in containers.

- THE RIGHT ROOTSTOCK
  Apples
  Pears
  Plums, damsons, peaches,
    apricots and nectarines
  Cherries

- SPECIAL SHAPES

THE RIGHT ROOTSTOCK

To get the most out of your space, grow fruit trees such as apples, pears and plums grafted onto dwarfing root stock. They double-up as productive plants and decorative features, such as 45 cm (18 in) or knee-high step-over hedges, or train them into shapes against walls or fences. Tree fruit such as apples, pears and figs will need to be potted on from time to time into larger containers, until finally they are in containers with a diameter of 45 cm (18 in) and at least 45 cm (18 in) deep.

When you order a tree check its rootstock. Apples (*Malus sylvestris* var. *domestica)*, plums (*Prunus domestica)*, pears (*Pyrus communis* var. *sativa*) and cherries (*Prunus cerasifera* and *Prunus avium*) are grafted onto rootstocks, which control their growth rate and their final size.

- **Apples** Rootstocks for apples are identified with the initial M and a number. This refers to East Malling and Long Ashton Research Stations where the original work on rootstocks was carried out. M9 is a dwarfing rootstock, M26 is a semi-dwarfing rootstock used for bush, espaliers and some upright-growing or columnar trees. These trees are useful as screens but they can also be grown in containers. M27 is a dwarfing rootstock, ideal for plants grown as cordons.

- **Pears** are grown on Quince A and B rootstocks.

- **Plums, damsons, peaches, apricots and nectarines** are on St Julien A rootstock. Pixy is a dwarfer rootstock for plums and damsons.

△ Apples can be trained into many shapes that will add architectural focus to the small garden and supply a good harvest of fruit. The branches of the tree are tied onto the metal hoops of a pre-formed globe, the upright of which is secured to the tree trunk for support.

SPECIAL SHAPES

There are a number of specially developed columnar shapes which are sold under a variety of trade names such as Pillarette and Minarette. These are specially suited to container growing or small-space gardens as a number of these upright trees can be grown in a small area. Some have two varieties of apples grafted onto them, offering you double the choice in a small space.

There are also a number of techniques which are used to train fruit trees into space-saving shapes. These include cordons, double cordons, fans, espaliers, pyramids, half-standards and step-overs. Two new systems where the trees are grown in V-shaped shows or trained into curved S-shapes encourage better fruit production and reduce the space needed in traditional planting systems.

△ **Cordons** are single-stemmed trees planted at a sloping angle, with their branches trained on wires. Although each plant produces less fruit, you can grow several along the edge of a path or as a hedge to enclose a garden.

△ **Espaliers** are trained so their branches grow in horizontal pairs from the main stem along wires or a wall. The main stem is upright and the trees can be taken to whatever height you wish, but need to rise in even pairs of branches.

△ **Step-over hedges** are really mini-espalier systems, with one pair of branches growing horizontally from the main stem. Their height of 30–45 cm (12–18 in) makes them a decorative as well as productive hedge for a small vegetable garden.

• **Cherries** Tabel is a dwarfing rootstock for cherries, keeping them to a height of 1.8–2.4 m (6–8 ft).

GARDENER'S TIP

When buying trees, choose varieties that will be good neighbours, providing pollen to swap via bees so that the fruits appear in abundance.

▷ Apple 'Discovery' trained into a mini-espalier system provides a seasonal display of flowers, followed by shiny fruits. At just 45 cm (18 in) high, this system described as a 'step-over' hedge, offers the twin opportunities of ornament and productivity so prized by small-space fruit growers.

CHOOSING
fruit trees

Choose fruit trees that the growers identify as having good pest- and disease-resistance and avoid those varieties that could pose problems.

- AVOIDING PROBLEMS
- POLLINATORS FOR APPLES
- PLANTING FRUIT TREES
- AWAITING FRUIT

AVOIDING PROBLEMS

There are also other ways in which you can control the likelihood of potential trouble.

• Mulching the ground around the tree's base and feeding it with a good fertilizer or with a fish, blood and bone mix are two ways of promoting health and vigour, raising its resistance to attack.

• Mulching to prevent soil moisture loss is also an effective and relatively simple way to control bitter pit in apples (spotting just beneath the skin of the fruit and pits on the skin surface) which is caused by calcium deficiency during times of drought.

• Control the spread of brown rot on fruit by taking off any affected fruits, otherwise this fungal condition will move through each cluster quickly (do not compost affected fruit).

• Although young trees need protection from excessive wind in their early years, a good circulation of air and an open, light site will go a long way to reduce pest and disease levels. Basic hygiene, such as keeping the site clean and free of diseased leaves and fruits, helps to keep the tree in good health.

POLLINATORS FOR APPLES

Most fruit nurseries indicate suitable pollinators by number or initials. So choose trees shown in catalogues as having the same number or letter grouping. Trees from the immediate neighbouring groups can also be chosen, as they will have enough of an overlapping flowering period to pollinate each other. Some types of apple are

△ In warm, sheltered gardens you can grow peaches in the ground or in containers. An ideal position would be against a south or south-west-facing wall. Peaches flower early in the growing season so provide frost protection for their blossoms.

described as poor pollinators, so you will need to grow two others from the relevant groups to keep the pollen going round for the fruit to set. In a small kitchen garden, these varieties are probably best avoided.

PLANTING FRUIT TREES

Once you have chosen the shape and varieties you want to grow, order the trees from specialist growers and nurseries. If you buy trees 3–4 years old, they will already be pruned into a good shape and you will only need to prune to produce fruiting branches. Bare-rooted apples are traditionally planted in late autumn to early spring, depending on soil conditions.

1 Prepare the site well by removing all perennial weeds and digging the soil to get it well aerated.

2 Make a planting hole for each of your trees, large enough to spread the roots into. The depth of the hole depends on the height of the soil mark on the stem. This enables you to keep the union (where the rootstock and grafted stem join) above soil level.

3 Knock a strong stake into the ground, so that it is firmly in place and its head is just below the first branches of the tree.

4 Fill the planting hole with the topsoil you have removed, mixed with compost and bonemeal.

5 Once the tree is in place in the planting hole, tie it to the stake. Water the tree in well after planting and all through the first spring and summer see that they are well watered.

Columnar trees in the Minarette and Pillarette ranges can be planted fairly close to each other at a distance of 60 cm (2 ft). They will crop when they reach a height of 1.8–2.4 m (6–8 ft).

AWAITING FRUIT

Young trees should not be allowed to fruit in their first year, so you will have to remove blossom in the first year after planting. This encourages the tree to put its energy into establishing good roots

△ Upright apple trees are useful in the border and are also suited to containers. Sold as 'Minarettes' or 'Pillarettes', they crop well and if grown against a wall can be netted to prevent bird damage to blossoms.

▷ Citrus trees offer fragrance and ornament from their scented flowers while their glossy foliage and decorative fruits are additional attributes. They should be brought inside at the first mention of frost.

and a strong structure, and stimulates it to produce abundant flowers and fruit next year.

Citrus, nectarines and peaches also suit container growing in sheltered and sunny gardens and on sheltered patios. Bring citrus trees inside during winter in cold temperate climates.

GROWING SOFT
fruit

Home-grown and fresh, soft fruit must surely be one of the most delicious and eagerly awaited harvests to come from the kitchen garden during the summer months.

- CHOOSING VARIETIES
   Raspberries and blackberries
   Currants
   Blueberries

- PRACTICALITIES

Soft fruits, including blackberries, red- and whitecurrants, gooseberries, raspberries, strawberries and many others, supply the extra ingredients that round off a summer's day meal.

Although soft fruits are usually grown in netted cages to protect them from birds, they can be just as successfully grown in smaller quantities mixed with herbs and vegetables in a potager, or even as decorative shrubs within a mixed border.

CHOOSING VARIETIES

There are many disease-resistant cultivars, as well as early- or late-fruiting varieties to choose.

- **Raspberries and blackberries** Plants such as raspberries and blackberries, known as cane fruit, are suckering and rambling plants respectively. Without support they would sprawl and scramble. Give them support, and use them and their supports to make a fruitful and ornamental hedge in part of the kitchen garden or as a screen against a shed wall.

- **Currants** are woody shrubs and can be grown in rows, mixed into a border or as centrepieces in a herb and vegetable patch.

- **Blueberries** are also woody shrubs, and need acid soil, so if you haven't the right soil conditions, grow them in ericaceous (lime-free) compost in large containers in a sheltered, but sunny site on a patio. You will need to grow two varieties to ensure pollination. In acid soil conditions they make a useful addition to a rhododendron and azalea planting. Their spring

△ Red- and white-currants can be grown in various space-saving shapes including cordons. This redcurrant 'Redstart' has been trained into a double cordon shape against a wall.

flowers are followed by fruits in summer and the attractive foliage makes a good autumnal show.

Using soft fruit ornamentally means that you are growing less for unlimited produce and more for beauty. You can only plant a few fruit bushes or canes, just sufficient to fill the space available, and you need to take extra care if you apply insecticide to the fruit bushes. The benefits of this type of double use are that you will have sufficient fruit to enjoy, and they will provide attraction with their shape, flowers and fruit.

PRACTICALITIES

If you are using the site as a mixed kitchen and ornamental garden, you will have prepared the soil sufficiently to support the fruit bushes' needs. In such a well-dug, well-composted site, in free-draining soil, they will have the basics necessary for good growth. You may still need to net them if birds compete with you for the harvest. If you have the space for a separate fruit cage, you can group soft fruit together, making it easier to protect the fruit from bird damage. If you cannot net the whole area, net individual plants using a temporary framework of canes to support the netting.

△ A framework of canes supports netting to provide temporary protection for individual trees from greedy birds.

◁ Red- and whitecurrants and gooseberries can be trained into half-standards, offering the small-space gardener attractive focal features and abundant fruit.

GROWING
strawberries

Strawberries are among the most evocative of summer fruits and, to my mind, no kitchen garden is complete without a pot or two.

- THE PLANTS
- MAKING SPACE
- PLANTING
- TABLE-TOP SYSTEM

THE PLANTS

Strawberries are herbaceous perennials that spread by making daughter plants at the end of long runners sent out from the main plant. You can either pot up the new plants or discard them if the existing plants are providing enough fruit.

Strawberries grow to form ground-covering mounds and can be used to make informal edging rows or ground cover in a mixed border.

MAKING SPACE

In conventional gardens strawberries take up a great deal of ground space, but the inventive small-space grower can grow them in pots. Strawberries can also be grown in specially made barrels or terracotta planters. The latest

method, known as the table-top method, is on raised strawberry platforms in grow-bags (see right) or wide windowbox-style containers.

Instead of growing strawberries in rows, plant them on either side of a path through the kitchen garden. Position them at least 30 cm (12 in) away from the edge of the bed. In summer when they flower and fruits begin to form, put in place a layer of straw around the plants to keep the fruits off the soil and free from dirt in wet conditions.

PLANTING

Water newly bought strawberry plants or soak bare-rooted plants in water before planting, but get them into their growing site as soon as possible. Set the plants about 30 cm (12 in) apart

△ Specially shaped terracotta pots with scooped-out planting pouches are a popular choice for growing strawberries in limited spaces. Take care when watering not to flush out compost from the top or pouches.

▷ Alpine strawberries fruit over a long period from late summer through to late autumn. The sweet, fragrant fruits are smaller than other varieties, and they are ideal for growing as informal edges for borders or as productive groundcover.

and plant them into a 15 cm (6 in) planting hole. Make sure there is space in the hole for the roots to fit. Weed around the plants regularly.

Strawberries, especially alpine strawberries, can also be grown in special tower containers on patios, and more for ornament than serious fruit, in hanging baskets. Many delicious varieties are available, including 'Cambridge Favourite', 'Elsanta' and 'Cambridge Late Pine', as well as more ornamental forms including a pink flowered strawberry, *Fragaria* 'Pink Panda' and a variegated leaf form, *Fragaria variegata*.

GARDENER'S TIP

Alpine strawberries (Fragaria vesca), with smaller leaves and more compact growth, make neat edges for borders and paths and provide sweeter fruits.

TABLE-TOP SYSTEM

Commercial strawberry growers have developed a raised system for growing strawberries en masse. There are kits available for home use. The idea is to grow the fruits at table height so they are easier to harvest and as the fruit is well off the ground there is no chance that it will get mud splashed, nor will it be necessary to raise fruit on a layer of straw. You can improvise with a slightly lower 'table-top' system by setting a plank on two or three breeze blocks. Use a grow-bag as the growing medium, cutting holes in the plastic on its top and inserting short canes at an angle to the grow-bag to hold some of the fruiting stems apart, so that they all ripen well.

SHRUBBY
fruits

Gooseberries, red- and whitecurrants and their hybrids can also be fitted into a mixed planting scheme, but they will need regular pruning to keep fruiting well.

- GOOSEBERRIES
- REDCURRANTS
- BLACKCURRANTS
- BLUEBERRIES
- FROST PROTECTION

Currants and gooseberries are available as stool bushes, where the stems come straight from the root system or as bushes with a leg and several stems growing from it. These plants can be trained into fan shapes to grow against walls, fences or the sides of garden buildings or they can be pruned into roughly U-shaped bushes, where their centres are open and allow good air circulation.

GOOSEBERRIES

Gooseberries *(Ribes grossularia)* are also available, or can be trained, as taller standards with round heads.

These are useful in an ornamental sense to provide height and raise eye-level in a low-level herb or kitchen garden.

Choices: 'Careless' and 'Invicta' have well-deserved reputations as heavy cropping and vigorous growing plants, and 'Invicta' is immune to mildew. 'Whinham's Industry' produces good-flavoured fruit and the extra attraction is that the fruit ripens to a dark red.

REDCURRANTS

Redcurrant *(Ribes vulgare)* fruits hang from the plant in clusters, like glistening red and white jewels.

Choices: The best choice for redcurrants

△ Redcurrant 'Stanza' produces small, dark red fruits that hang in glossy trusses on upright, shrubby bushes.

is 'Rovada', with large clusters of fruit in late summer. 'Jonkheer van Tets' and 'Stanza' also provide abundant fruit in late summer. For variation grow whitecurrant 'White Versailles'. The fruits gleam like large yellowish raindrops on the bushes and are ready to pick in summer.

Prune gooseberries and currants to keep an open shape, with good air circulation at the centre of the plant. The plants should look like a goblet or vase in outline. Once you have the shape, prune

off two-thirds of the length of remaining branches, to leave a pair of buds going to the left and right of the stem. Remove any suckers that appear at the base of the plants in summer, by simply pulling them off the plant.

BLACKCURRANTS

Blackcurrants *(Ribes nigrum)* can be used to make a simple hedge at the edge of a vegetable plot. At the time of planting cut stems back to buds at about 5–10 cm (2–4 in) above ground level. In later years, when plants are growing well, cut back fruiting stems when you harvest and others by a third. **Choices:** Many disease- and frost-resistant cultivars exist, including 'Ben Sarek'.

spindly stems and those that cross. Otherwise only take out up to a quarter of stems that have fruited each year. **Choices:** 'Bluecrop' grows into an upright shape and will do well in dry or

△ Blueberry 'Bluecrop'.

well-drained, but moist conditions. 'Coville' ripens late in the season, while 'Earliblue' is at its best in midsummer.

BLUEBERRIES

Blueberries *(Vaccinium* spp.) need acid soil conditions to fruit well. If your soil conditions are not suitable, provided you have the space for two varieties (necessary for good pollination), you can grow them in large pots in the garden or on a patio. If you do have acid soil conditions, blueberry bushes will look attractive in spring with their tiny white bell flowers, be productive in summer and in autumn their foliage will provide burnished colour.

Blueberry plants can grow up to 1.5–1.8 m (5–6 ft) and take a number of years before they fruit. Some are self-fertile, but planting two varieties ensures better pollination.

Prune blueberry bushes once they are well-established, after four years. For the first pruning, take out weak and

FROST PROTECTION

Wall- or fence-trained fruit trees, such as cherries, peaches and apples will benefit from frost protection, which should increase fruit production.

1 Fix a wooden batten to the wall above the tree and tack material such as horticultural fleece, hessian or plastic into place. Keep it away from the tree by laying a few canes against the underside of the batten, with the lower ends of the canes pushed into the ground.

2 Tie the vertical sides of the material onto the canes and weight the bottom end on the ground using stones or bricks. By day, move the fabric off the blossoms so they can be pollinated.

GROWING CANE
fruits

Raspberries, blackberries, Japanese wineberries and hybrids, such as loganberry, sunberry, tummelberry and tayberry, need strong and permanent supports for their rambling or whippy fruiting stems.

- RASPBERRIES
- BLACKBERRIES
- HYBRID BERRIES

RASPBERRIES

The raspberry (Rubus idaeus) offers luscious fruits in summer and in autumn. The autumn fruits come from new season's growth, so cut canes right to the ground each winter to produce new canes that won't fruit in summer, but will be ready in autumn.

A group of 4–6 raspberry canes, supported by tall bamboo canes, makes a centrepiece for a formal kitchen garden that is both decorative and productive. Tie the fruit canes into the bamboo canes at regular intervals, and make sure the supporting structure is secure, by tying the bamboo canes

together with lightweight garden wire.
Choices: Best summer fruit choices are 'Glen Cova' and 'Glen Moy' with 'Golden Everest', a yellow-fruiting form. Raspberries that fruit in autumn, bringing all the fragrance of summer-fruiting cultivars, include 'Autumn Bliss', 'Fallgold' and 'Zeva'.

BLACKBERRIES

Blackberries (Rubus fruticosus) grow best in full sun in well-drained but moist sites. Enrich the soil before planting with well-rotted manure. Set the plants in place at the base of the fencing or support system and cut the plants back

△ Raspberry canes frame an archway on a grape-shaded patio.

to 20 cm (8 in). As the canes grow, train them into the supports and each year, in winter cut out the canes that fruited during the year. Mulch the soil around the base of the plants with compost to reduce weeds and to retain moisture. In dry seasons water the bushes as the berries begin to turn purple.
Choices: 'Fantasia' is a new variety of blackberry growing on a vigorous plant which bears very heavily and has good flavour, tasting very much like the wild blackberry. 'Loch Ness' is a thornless,

△ Blackberry 'Fantasia'.

well-flavoured blackberry which crops well. 'Oregon Thornless' has all the attributes of cultivated blackberries but in addition provides attractive autumnal foliage colour. For attractive flowers grow 'Veronique' which has pink blooms and is thornless.

HYBRID BERRIES

The hybrid berries are crosses between blackberries and raspberries and other *Rubus* species. They vary in colour, from purple through to pink and red. Blackberries and their hybrid berries (which include the loganberry, silvanberry, sunberry, tayberry and tummelberry) are all heavy-cropping and good-tasting. They can be used in similar decorative and productive ways to produce summer fruits. However, they all need space, in most cases

about 2.4 m (8 ft), so unless you have a long fence to cover, it is likely that you will only be able to fit one or two plants into a kitchen garden.

In a mixed planting, though, you can use these plants for ornamental effect, or even practical purposes, to make a slim and productive hedge for part of the garden. Positioned well, the fruit

'hedge' may form a boundary between different parts of the garden. Blackberries and their hybrids and the Japanese wineberry can be trained over arched supports or wound around the pillars of a pergola.

▽ Loganberries, which are blackberry hybrids, produce sharp-tasting fruits.

There are some layouts that suit kitchen gardens particularly well, and these can be easily adapted to fit individual situations. The idea is to get the most out of every bit of bare earth, patio or rooftop.

6

garden
plans

A VEGETABLE CIRCLE GARDEN

A SEMI-CIRCULAR VEGETABLE GARDEN

A POTAGER-STYLE GARDEN

A ROOFTOP CONTAINER GARDEN

A FRUIT GARDEN

◁ Maximize the productivity of every part of the garden, supporting climbing vegetables such as beans on canes that become an intrinsic part of the garden's style.

A VEGETABLE CIRCLE garden

Circles are popular shapes for ornamental flower gardens and herb gardens, and in the small garden they suit vegetable growing well. A circle can be divided into diamond or wedge-shaped sections, and further sub-divided into smaller sections for planting small quantities of a particular vegetable and for successional sowing. The overall outline is of a wheel, with divisions that resemble the spokes of a wheel. A circular bed is easy to see at a glance, and its shape allows you easy access for weeding and harvesting from the outer edges. However, when you need to work at the centre of the circle you should avoid walking directly on the soil, so allow space for either stepping stones or narrow paths for you to tread on.

• **The layout** The circular plot shown here has a diameter of 3 m (10 ft) and is divided into an inner and outer circle, with a central planting area holding a collection of runner beans, and providing a decorative focal point for the circle. Using string and wooden pegs, divide the circle into six segments. Similarly, with a shorter piece of string mark out the circumference of the inner circle.

The outer circle has stepping stones placed at regular intervals in between the vegetable sections. By

◁ Grow as much as you can within the confines of the circular vegetable garden by using the central area to grow a climbing crop. You can either use traditional supports, a typical garden object such as a climbing frame or even an old ladder to hold the tough stems and heavy fruits of squash or pumpkin.

standing on them you can weed and maintain the inner circle of vegetables without compacting the soil.

• **The wigwam** Put in place the canes for the central bean wigwam. Push the ends firmly into the ground so that the structure is stable and tie the tops securely in place. Wind string around the wigwam at intervals up the length

of the canes, to provide additional footholds for the climbing beans.

• **Planting** You can choose to grow varying amounts of a particular vegetable within each segment or its subdivision. As one small block of vegetables is harvested you can replace it with seeds, seedlings, or young plants of a second crop.

PLANTING THE VEGETABLE CIRCLE

FOR THE CENTRE

① **Beans:** there are at least six canes, with three plants per cane (one on each side of the cane) – 'Relay' which has white, pink and red flowered varieties in the seed mix, 'Cosse Violette' (purple pods), 'Corona d'Oro' (yellow pods), 'Painted Lady' (pretty white and red flowers) and 'Blue Lake' (green pods). Surround the bean wigwam with a circle of parsley and chives or spring onions.

OUTER PARTS OF THE CIRCLE

② **Lettuces:** grow several varieties, varying them as you harvest. Grow six blush-types with purple/green markings such as 'Little Leprechaun', six cos types such as 'Little Gem' and six oakleaf types such as 'Red Salad Bowl' or 'Salad Bowl' (green leaves). Follow lettuces with winter leeks.

③ **Turnips:** two rows of 'Atlanta', followed by spicy oriental greens, mizuna and mustard 'Red Giant', which will over-winter.

④ **Carrots:** grow two rows near the centre of the outer circle, with nine onion sets at the edge of the circle or six, if larger onions are wanted.

⑤ **Chard:** grow two rows selecting from Swiss chard (green foliage and stems), Ruby Chard (red) or Bright Lights (rainbow colours in stems and leaves).

⑥ **Radish:** sown in a random broadcast of seed, followed in summer by one or, at most, two courgette plants.

⑦ **Beetroot:** grow two rows of 'Chioggia Pink' or 'Boltardy'.

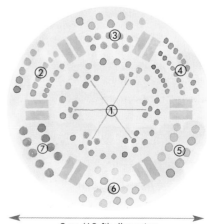

3 m (10 ft) diameter

A SEMI-CIRCULAR vegetable garden

Using a circular shape as its basis, the semi-circle enables you to take advantage of odd areas in the garden and you could even extend it into a three-quarter circle, butting onto a path or against the side of the house. This is also a perfect shape to use against the back wall of a town garden.

• **Marking out** To mark it out, put in place two canes at either end of the straight, back edge of the semi-circle. Mark the middle, put a cane in place and then with a piece of string half the length of the straight side, mark out the circumference of the semi-circle.

• **Edgings and paths** Edge the bed with a path for ease of access. It is also useful to have a stepping stone or chequer-board path at the rear if the semi-circle backs onto a wall or fence so you can work at the back of the bed without compacting the soil. In any case, the area immediately by the wall will be dry, making it difficult to grow vegetables close up to it. If you use a chequer-board, stepping stone approach to the path at the back, plant herbs such as chives, oregano and thyme into the spaces between the pavers or stepping stones. Put in place a few stepping stones within the bed itself, so that you can have easy access without damaging plants and soil by treading on them.

• **Planting** The semi-circle is roughly divided into segments, but some crops are planted in rows that cross several segment divisions. At the centre and to the back of the semi-circle, to give height and a focal point, grow runner beans supported on canes. Instead of arranging canes in a traditional wigwam shape, you could vary the central

△ Arrange canes in a short row that follows the lines of a semi-circular plan to contrast with the curves at the front of the garden.

focus by growing the beans in a short row, placing the canes in a line. Leave enough space between the beans and the back wall to enable you to get behind the canes to harvest the crop.

PLANT LIST

① Chives

② Oregano

③ Thyme

④ Chervil

⑤ Runner beans 'Painted Lady' and 'Relay' for a variety of flower colour

⑥ Swiss chard ('Bright Lights' for multi-coloured effect or plain green 'Lucullus' or red 'Burgundy Chard')

⑦ Ornamental cabbage (colourful, edible varieties are available)

⑧ Onion sets 'New Fen Globe'

⑨ Sprouting broccoli (green 'Early White Sprouting' and purple form 'Early Purple Sprouting')

⑩ Carrots 'Parmex' or 'Parabell'

⑪ Beetroot 'Boltardy' or 'Monogram'

⑫ Radish 'Cherry Belle' or 'Scarlet Globe' (once harvested, sow more lettuce or Oriental greens)

⑬ Lettuce (mixed plantings of different colours) 'Salad Bowl' (green), 'Little Leprechaun' (mauve/purple)

⑭ Two courgette plants (one green form 'Ambassador' and one yellow-skinned form 'Taxi', 'Gold Rush' or 'Jemmer').

⑮ Oriental greens (broadcast seed)

⑯ Two peppers 'Big Banana' (plant out only when all danger of frost is over)

⑰ Two tomatoes 'Golden Sunrise' and 'Sweet Cherry'

A POTAGER-STYLE garden

Angular shapes, such as triangles and squares, are popular choices for containing formal vegetable gardens. Each bed is in essence a raised bed, edged with boards and filled with soil and compost. This design can be used as part of a rotation where you move crops from square to square annually.

If space permits you can fit all four squares into your garden; if not reduce the number of squares to two and divide each into four, so that you can still grow the same range of vegetables, even if in smaller quantities.

• **The layout** The four squares in this formal vegetable garden are divided by a path 45–60 cm (1½–2 ft) wide – broad enough to work from and to push a wheelbarrow along. When laying out the garden, measure out the beds and secure the treated wooden boards in place, then add the soil and compost to each bed and fork it over well, allowing it to settle before planting up.

• **Making the paths** Remove stones and weeds from the area which is to become the paths and lay a woven plastic membrane. This dark material blocks out light and weakens any weed

seedlings or perennial weeds that start to grow. On top of the membrane add a layer of gravel or bark to reduce the likelihood of weed seedlings coming through and to provide a finished, ornamental look to the design. The membrane is permeable so water will filter through, becoming available in the soil for the vegetable plants.

▽ Although the boards enclosing the raised beds will hold most plants away from the paths, you can ensure that large vegetable foliage is held off by placing low, decorative hoops or hurdles inside the boards.

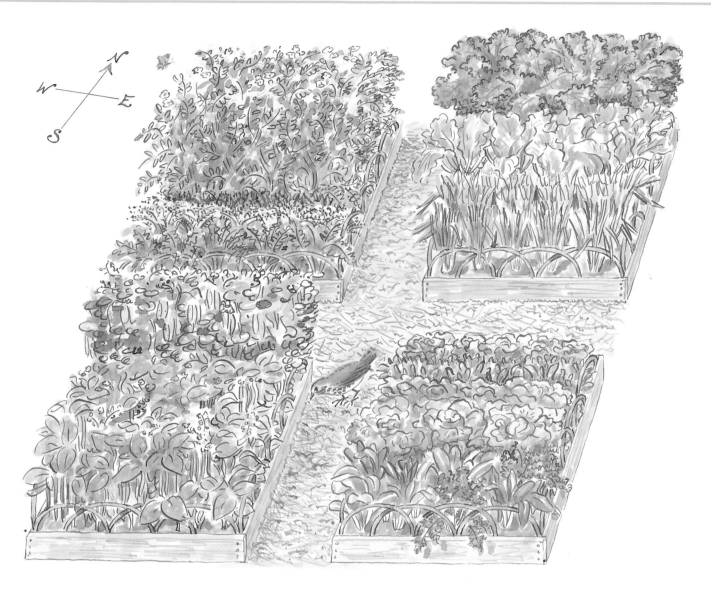

PLANTING THE POTAGER-STYLE GARDEN

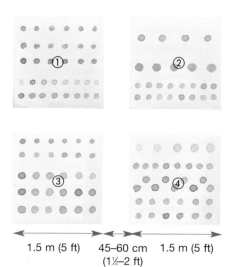

1.5 m (5 ft)   45–60 cm   1.5 m (5 ft)
                (1½–2 ft)

① **Roots**
Three rows of potatoes 'Mimi' or
    'Dunluce'.
One row of carrots 'Early Market'.
One row of parsnip 'Tender and True'.

② **Brassicas and onions**
Kale 'Redbor' (one row taking up
    45 cm/18 in).
Kohlrabi 'Purple Delicacy' and 'Green
    Delicacy'.
Two rows of onions 'Centurion'.

③ **Peas and beans**
Double row of sugar peas 'Sugar
    Rae', with twigs in place to support
    the crop as it grows.
Three rows of dwarf French beans in a
    range of pod colours: 'Royalty'
    (purple), 'Canadian Wonder' (green)
    and 'Sungold' (yellow).

④ **Salads and Chinese greens**
Lettuce 'Red Salad Bowl' or 'Marvel of
    Four Seasons'.
Salad rocket.
Several rows of mixed lettuces and
    cut-and-come-again mixtures.
Two rows of Chinese greens (mizuna,
    mibuna, purple mustard, Pak Choi).

A ROOFTOP container garden

Even in the confined spaces of a rooftop, it is possible to grow a range of vegetables and herbs that will provide both tasty produce and ornamental qualities. You will not be able to grow in quantity, but by choosing the vegetables you like most you will be able to keep a succession going, bringing on new plants for those already harvested.

• **Containers** The secret of success lies in having the largest containers you can safely site on the roof or balcony. You may need to reinforce the roof and for this you will need professional advice. Large containers offer more space in this already space-hungry site, but they don't need watering daily, which reduces maintenance. However, size does mean weight, so be sure you have the container sited correctly before you fill it with compost.

If safety constraints and access allow, put in place raised, waist-high planting systems which run around the outline of the roof. You could also group containers together, in same-plant selections or in a random arrangement of vegetables, in much the same way as you would plan a decorative collection.

• **Grow-bags** Some containers, such as grow-bags, are functional

and not overly attractive, but if they fulfil their use well, they are forgiven their looks. Watering can be a problem, as water usually spills out of the planting holes bringing with it some of the compost. If using grow-bags for tomatoes, avoid this by planting them in bottomless pots and sinking these into the grow-bag. When you water, aim the hose or watering can into the pot rather than into the grow-bag itself.

• **Space** Space is naturally at a premium so plantings go upwards as well as horizontal, and hanging baskets and windowboxes are essential elements of

▷ Grow fruit trees including apples, peaches and citrus in a sheltered position on the balcony or patio.

◁ Tomato 'Sun Belle' is a mini-plum tomato with a sweet flavour that grows well in containers.

the rooftop garden. They must be securely fixed if they overhang the street or a neighbour's patio or balcony.

• **Shelter** On a rooftop or balcony wind may cause problems, so some form of shelter will be needed. You can fix trellis on a batten and secure this on the inside of the exterior wall of the roof, so that it is higher than the wall. Similarly, glass screens secured in place, although expensive, will reduce the vigour of the wind and increase the warmth of the site, without losing the views around it.

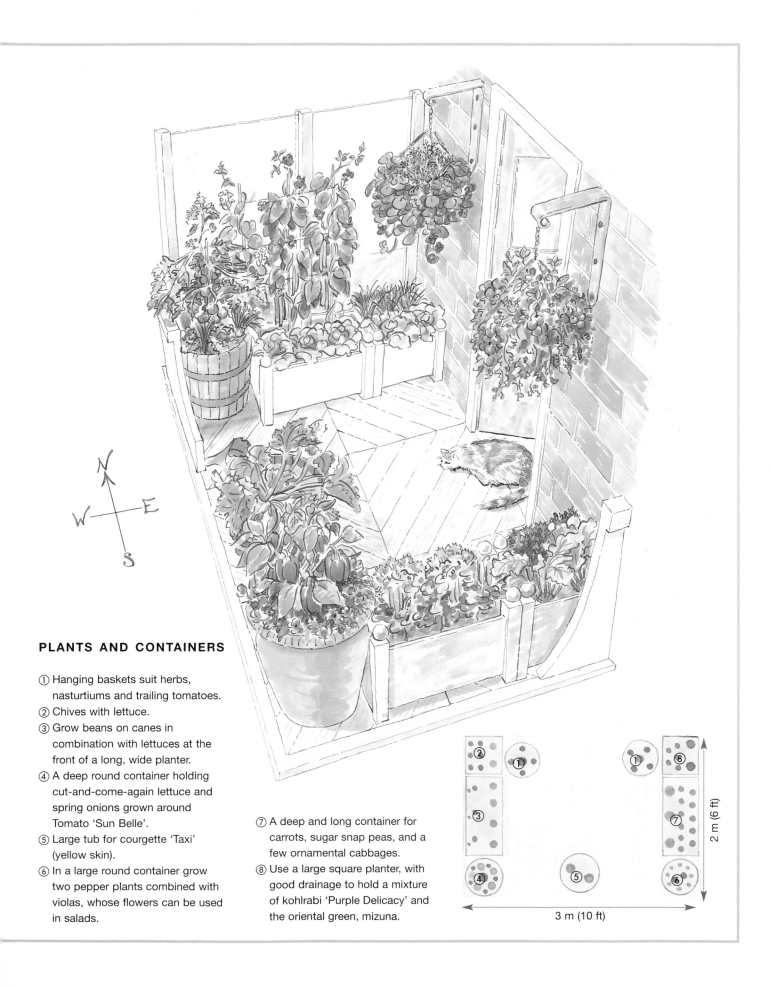

PLANTS AND CONTAINERS

① Hanging baskets suit herbs, nasturtiums and trailing tomatoes.

② Chives with lettuce.

③ Grow beans on canes in combination with lettuces at the front of a long, wide planter.

④ A deep round container holding cut-and-come-again lettuce and spring onions grown around Tomato 'Sun Belle'.

⑤ Large tub for courgette 'Taxi' (yellow skin).

⑥ In a large round container grow two pepper plants combined with violas, whose flowers can be used in salads.

⑦ A deep and long container for carrots, sugar snap peas, and a few ornamental cabbages.

⑧ Use a large square planter, with good drainage to hold a mixture of kohlrabi 'Purple Delicacy' and the oriental green, mizuna.

2 m (6 ft)

3 m (10 ft)

A FRUIT garden

If fruit is your preference, it is possible to fill a small garden and an adjoining patio with a sufficient variety of fruits to provide delicious produce as well as ornament in the form of flowers, fruit and, very often, autumn foliage.

• **The layout** The design shown here is for a 10 x 10 m (30 x 30 ft) plot and would fill the whole of a typical urban back garden, being both productive and highly attractive.

The suntrap of the patio allows you to grow fan-trained nectarine and cherry on opposite walls and a grapevine trained against the wall and over the back door. Figs and blueberry plants are grown in large wooden containers such as half-barrels and strawberries are grown in waist-high, table-top containers. The edge of the paved patio is lined with a low-growing, step-over planting of apples, separated by a central wrought iron archway, which supports a blackberry on one side and a boysenberry on the other, leading out into the garden.

Lining a path or simply planted into beds cut out of the grass is a row of fruit trees grown as half standards, including whitecurrants, redcurrants, pinkcurrants and gooseberries.

At the end of the line of half standards is an arbour with a fan-trained cherry on the back wall. Two lemon verbenas, grown as standards, are in pots at the edge of the arbour area, which can be underplanted with thyme, which will release its aroma as you walk over the foliage.

Growing along the two sides of the fruit garden are a collection of apples and pears to the left, and on the right a selection of raspberries. On the far boundary of the garden, against the wall or fence are tayberries, jostaberries and a blackcurrant, while a Victoria plum completes the tree fruit selection in the far corner on the right-hand side.

◁ If fruit is your delight, every available surface including walls and fences will become a site for training plants such as this fan-shaped morello cherry.

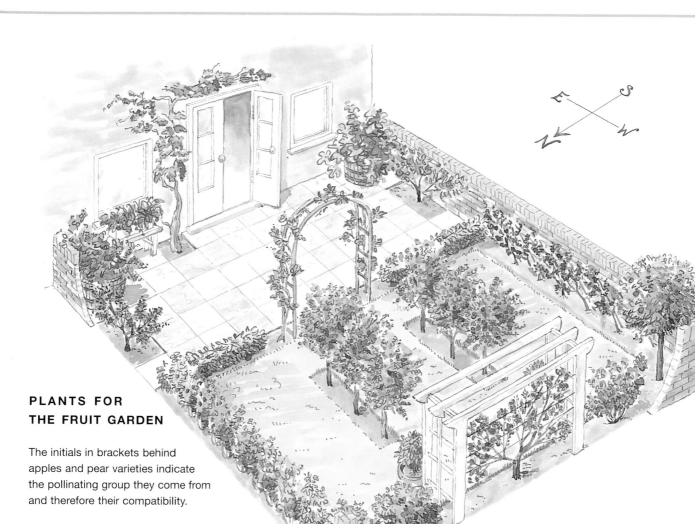

PLANTS FOR THE FRUIT GARDEN

The initials in brackets behind apples and pear varieties indicate the pollinating group they come from and therefore their compatibility.

① Patio

1 Fig

2 Grape

3 Strawberries: six plants of *Fragaria variegata* and six plants of 'Cambridge Late Pine'

4 Blueberry 'Earliblue'

4 Blueberry 'Coville'

5 Fan-trained cherry 'Morello'

6 Fan-trained nectarine 'Lord Napier'

7 Step-over apple hedge 'Lord Derby' (c)

8 Step-over apple hedge 'Charles Ross' (B)

② Arch

9 Boysenberry

10 Blackberry

③ Left-hand boundary

11 Apple 'Worcester Pearmain' (B)

12 Pear 'William' (C)

13 Pear 'Doyenne' (D)

14 Pear 'Beth' (D)

15 Pear 'Concorde' (C)

16 Apple 'Howgate Wonder' (C)
These are grown as cordons on a post and fence system, spaced 75 cm (2 ft 6 in apart)

④ Back wall

17 Plum 'Victoria'

18 Tayberry 'Buckingham'

19 Fan-trained cherry 'Stella'

20 Lemon verbena grown as standards in containers

21 Jostaberry

22 Blackcurrant 'Ben Sarek'

⑤ Right-hand boundary

23 Raspberry 'Autumn Bliss': five plants

24 Raspberry 'Fall Gold': five plants

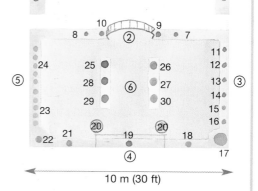

⑥ Row of half standards in lawn

25 Whitecurrant 'White Versailles'

26 Pinkcurrant 'Pink Jean'

27 Redcurrant 'Stanza'

28 Redcurrant 'Jonkheer van Tets'

29 Gooseberry 'Invicta'

30 Gooseberry 'Whinham's Industry'

FURTHER reading

Chef's Garden: Fresh Produce from Small Spaces,
Terence Conran (Conran Octopus, 1999)

Cool Green Leaves & Red Hot Peppers, Christine
McFadden and Michael Michaud (Frances Lincoln,
1998)

Creative Vegetable Gardening, Joy Larkcom (Mitchell
Beazley, 1997)

Heritage Vegetables, The Gardener's Guide to Cultivating
Diversity, Sue Stickland (Gaia Books Ltd, 1998)

Matthew Biggs's Complete Book of Vegetables (Kyle
Cathie Ltd, 1997)

Organic Gardening, Roy Lacey (David & Charles, 1988)

Pests: How to Control them on Fruit and Vegetables,
Pauline Pears and Bob Sherman (Henry Doubleday
Research Association/Search Press, 1992)

*RHS Pests & Diseases: The Complete Guide to
Preventing, Identifying and Treating Plant Problems*,
Pippa Greenwood and Andrew Halstead (Dorling
Kindersley, 1997)

Roof Gardens, Balconies & Terraces, Jerry Harpur and
David Stevens (Mitchell Beazley 1997)

The Container Garden Month-by-Month, Jackie Bennett
(David & Charles, 1994)

The Container Kitchen Garden, Antony Atha (Collins &
Brown, 2000)

The Edible Container Garden, Michael Guerra (Gaia
Books Ltd, 2000)

The Gardener's Guide to Organic Gardening, Editor
Valerie Duncan (Merehurst Ltd, 2000)

The Herb Garden Month-by-Month, Barbara Segall (David
& Charles, 1994)

The Kitchen Garden Month-by-Month, Andi Clevely
(David & Charles, 1996)

The New Kitchen Garden, Anna Pavord (Dorling
Kindersley, 1996)

Urban Eden, Adam and James Caplin (Kyle Cathie
Limited, 2000)

Vegetables, Ann Bonar (Tiger Books International, 1994)

Weeds: How to Control and Love Them, Jo Readman
(Henry Doubleday Research Association/Search Press,
1991)

Kitchen Garden Magazine
Subscription Dept, Warners, West Street, Bourne,
Lincolnshire PE10 9PH
Tel: 01778 391134

USEFUL addresses

GARDEN CENTRES AND SEED SUPPLIERS

UNITED KINGDOM

Chase Organics
The Organic Gardening Catalogue
Riverdene Business Park
Molesey Road
Horsham
Surrey KT12 4RG
Tel: (+44) (0)1932 253666
www.organiccatalog.com
E-mail: chaseorg@aol.com

Chiltern Seeds
Bortree Stile
Ulverston
Cumbria LA12 7PB
Tel : (+44) (0)1229 581 137
Fax: (+44) (0)1229 584 549
www.chilternseeds.co.uk

D T Brown & Co Ltd
Station Road
Poulton-le-Fylde
Lancashire FY6 7HX
Tel : (+44) (0)1253 882 371
Fax : (+44) (0)1253 890 923

Dobies
Long Road
Paignton
Devon TQ4 7SX
Tel: (+44) (0)1803 696444
Fax: (+44) (0)1803 696450
E-mail: gardening@dobies.co.uk
www.dobies.co.uk

Future Foods
PO Box 1564
Wedmore
Somerset BS28 4DP
Tel/Fax: (+44) (0)1934 713623
www.futurefoods.com

Halcyon Seeds
10 Hampden Close
Chalgrove
Oxford OX44 7SB
Tel/Fax : (+44) (0)1865 890180
www.halcyonseeds.co.uk

Highfield Nurseries
The Nursery
School Lane
Whitminstger
Gloucester GL2 7PL
Tel: (+44) (0)1452 740266
Fax: (+44) (0)1452 740750

Kings Seeds
Monks Farm
Kelvedon
Colchester
Essex CO5 9PG
Tel: (+44) (0)1376 570000
Fax: (+44) (0)1376 571189

S.E. Marshall & Co. Ltd
Wisbech
Cambridgeshire PE13 2RF
Tel: (+44) (0)1945 583407

Mr Fothergill's Seeds
Gazeley Road
Kentford
Newmarket
Suffolk CB8 7QB
Tel: (+44) (0)1638 552512
Fax: (+44) (0)1638 750468
www.mr-fothergills.co.uk

Ken Muir
Honeypot Farm
Rectory Road
Weeley Heath
Essex CO16 9BJ
Tel: (+44) (0)1255 830181
Fax: (+44) (0)1255 831534

Simpsons Seeds
27 Meadowbrook
Old Oxted
Surrey RH8 9LT
Tel: (+44) (0)1883 715242

Suffolk Herbs
Monks Farm
Coggeshall Road
Kelvedon
Essex CO5 9PG
Tel: (+44) (0)1376 572456
www.suffolkherbs@btinternet.com

Suttons
Woodview Road
Paignton
Devon TQ4 7NG
Tel: (+44) (0)1803 696300
Fax: (+44) (0)1803 696345

Terre de Semences
Ripple Farm
Crundale
Canterbury
Kent CT4 7EB
Tel: (+44) (0)1227 730790
www.terredesemences.com

Thompson & Morgan
Poplar Lane
Ipswich
Suffolk IP8 3BU
Tel: (+44) (0)1473 688588
Fax: (+44) (0)1473 680199
www.thompson-morgan.com

Unwins Seeds Limited
Histon
Cambridge CB4 9LE
Tel: (+44) (0)1223 236236
Fax: (+44) (0)1223 237437

UNITED STATES OF AMERICA

W Atlee Burpee & Co
300 Park Avenue
Warminster
PA 18974
Tel: (+1) 215 674 4900

Bountiful Gardens Seeds
18001 Shafer Ranch Road
Willits
CA 95490
Tel: (+1) 707 459 6410

Filaree Farm
Rt 2, Box 162
Okanogan
WA 98840
Tel: (+1) 509 422 6940

Johnny's Selected Seeds
Foss Hill Road
Albion
ME 04910
Tel: (+1) 207 437 9294
Fax: (+1) 207 437 2165

Seed Savers Exchange
3076 North Winn Road
Decorah, IA 52101
Tel: (+1) 319 382 5990
Fax: (+1) 319 382 587

AUSTRALIA

Michele Shennen's Garden Centre
427 Darling Street
Balmain
NSW 2041
Tel: (02) 9810 8892

Greengold Garden Centre
Banks Street
Weston Park
Yarralumla
ACT 2600
Tel: (02) 6281 7373

The Cottage Garden Nursery
999 Stanley St
East Brisbane
QLD 4169
Tel: (07) 3891 7999

Newman's Nursery
North East Road
Tea Tree Gully
SA 5091
Tel: (08) 8264 2661

Digger's Club and Digger's Mail
Order Seeds
Heronswood
105 La Trobe Parade
Dromana
VIC 3936
Tel: (03) 5987 1877
Fax: (03) 5981 4298
e-mail: info@diggers.com.au
www.diggers.com.au

NEW ZEALAND

Gardenways Garden Centres
Branches throughout Christchurch
Tel: (03) 385 3899 for nearest
location

Kings Plant Barn
Takapuna, Tel: (09) 443 2221
Remuera, Tel: (09) 524 9400
St Lukes, Tel: (09) 846 2141
Howick, Tel: (09) 273 8527
www.kings.co.nz

McCully's Garden Centres
Branches throughout Christchurch
Tel: (03) 3517128 for nearest
location

Nestlebrae Exotics
219 South Head Road
Parkhurst
Helensville
Tel: (09) 420 7312
www.helensville.co.nz/nestlebrae

Palmers Gardenworld
Head Office:
182 Wairau Road
Glenfield
Auckland
Tel: (09) 4439910
Freephone: 0800 PALMERS
www.palmersgardenworld.co.nz
*Branches throughout the North
Island*

Subtropical Nursery
PO Box 36 597
Northcote
Auckland
Tel: (09) 480 5148
Subtropical fruits catalogue

SOUTH AFRICA

Blackwoods Herbs
P.O. Box 6078
Uniedal
Cape Town 7612
Tel/Fax: (021) 889 1001

The Herb Farm
264 Uys Street
Randfield
Johannesburg 1501
Tel: (011) 425 2155
Fax: (011) 425 3662

Lifestyle Family Garden Centre
Corner of D.F Malan and Ysterhout
Avenue
P.O. Box 2568
Northcliff 2115
Tel: (011) 792 5616
Fax: (011) 792 5626

Plantpark Bryanston
278 Main Road
Bryanston 2021
Tel.: (011) 463 5773
Fax: (011) 463 5775
www.plantpark.co.za

Jesmond Dene Garden Pavillion
204 Murray Road
Hayfields
Pietermaritzburg 3201
Tel: (033) 396 5000
Fax: (033) 396 5100
www.jesmondene.active.com

Ninth Avenue Garden Centre
9th Avenue Shopping Centre
Walmer
Port Elizabeth 6070
Tel: (041) 955 5480
Fax: (041) 581 5343

Spitskop Garden Centre
P.O. Box 25069
Langenhoven Park 9330
Tel: (051) 451 1069
Fax: (051) 451 1193

ORGANIZATIONS

UNITED KINGDOM
**The Henry Doubleday Research
Association (HDRA)**
Henry Doubleday Foundation
Ryton Organic Gardens
Ryton-on-Dunsmore
Coventry CV8 3LG
Tel (+44) (0)24 7630 3517
Fax: (+44) (0)24 7663 9229
www.hdra.org.uk

The Royal Horticultural Society
80 Vincent Square
London SW1P 2PE
Tel: (+44) (0)20 7834 4333
Mail order: (+44) (0)1483 211320
www.rhs.org.uk

AUSTRALIA
**Organic Gardening and Farming
Society of Tasmania Inc.**
13 Guy Cresent
Somerset
TAS 7322
Tel: (+61) (3) 6435 1319
E-mail: OGFS@yahoo.com.au

Brisbane Organic Growers Inc.
PO Box 236
Lutwyche
Brisbane
QLD 4030
www.bog.powerup.com.au

**Canberra Organic Growers
Society (COGS)**
PO Box 347
Dickson
ACT 2602
E-mail: cogs@netspeed.com.au
www.netspeed.com.au/cogs

WEBSITES
www.expertgardener.com
www.edible.co.nz
www.garden-nz.co.nz
www.gardens.co.nz
www.living-earth.co.nz
www.naturalhub.com
www.plantfinder.co.nz
www.cityfarmer.org
www.garden.org
www.garden.co.za
www.prairienet.org
www.windowboxherbs.com
www.windowbox.com
www.growinglifestyle.com

INDEX

air circulation 14, 72
aphids 27
apples 92, 93
  in containers 17
  planting 73
  pollinators 72–3
  rootstocks 70–1
  step-over hedges 8, 36–7, 71
  training 71
apricots 71
aubergines 24, 44, 48, 59

baby vegetables 33, 66
balconies 16–17, 44, 45
basil 24, 48, 67
bay 67
beans 36, 62–3, 85, 89
  in containers 18, 91
  crop rotation 29
  supports 17, 38, 82
beds, raised 13, 17, 21, 34–5
beetroot 29, 35, 38, 65, 85, 87
birds 26, 74, 75
blackberries 12, 37, 38, 74, 80–1, 92, 93
blackcurrants 79, 92, 93
blackfly 27
blight 29
blueberries 37, 74–5, 79, 92, 93
borage 6
boysenberries 92, 93
brassicas 29, 54, 89
broad beans 12, 30, 63
broccoli 29, 59, 87
Brussels sprouts 54

cabbage root fly 27
cabbages 8, 29, 36, 37, 54, 87, 91
calcium 9, 72
canker 28
carrot fly 27
carrots 24, 29, 33, 35, 54, 64–5, 85, 87, 89, 91
caterpillars 28
cauliflowers 7, 29, 54
celery 30
chard 37, 57, 85
cherries 70, 71, 92, 93
chervil 49, 87
chicory 56
Chinese greens 89
chives 6, 12, 29, 36, 48, 67, 86, 87, 91
circle garden 84–5
citrus trees 73
climbing plants 38–9
cloches 32
close spacing 33
clubroot 29
companion planting 26
compost 15, 20, 22–3
containers 43–51
  grow-bags 48–9, 50, 90
  hanging baskets 48, 49, 50–1, 91
  patios and courtyards 18–19
  planting 46–7
  potting compost 21–2
  rooftop gardens 90–1
  sowing seed 24–5
  watering 23
  windowboxes 48, 50
cordons 8, 71
courgettes 24, 29, 48, 52, 60, 87, 91
courtyards 18–19
crop rotation 29

cucumbers 24, 48
curly kale 56–7

damping off 25, 29
damsons 71
decorative planting 36–9
digging 15, 20
dill 49
diseases 14, 26, 28–9, 45
downy mildew 29
drainage, containers 46
dwarf beans 12, 35, 62, 89

edgings 40
espaliers 71

fertilizers 20, 21, 72
figs 37, 70, 92, 93
flea beetles 28
fleece, horticultural 27
flowers, edible 67
four-square gardening 35
French beans 35, 62, 89
frost protection, fruit 79
fruit 69–81, 92–3
  cane fruit 80–1
  decorative planting 36–7
  frost protection 79
  planting 73
  pollinators 72–3
  rootstocks 70–1
  shrubby fruits 78–9
  soft fruit 74–5
  step-over hedges 8, 36–7, 71
  training 71
  trees 72–3

garlic 29
germination 24
gooseberries 37, 74, 75, 78, 92, 93
gourds 38, 60
grapes 38, 68, 92, 93
greenfly 27
greenhouses 13
grey mould 29
grow-bags 48–9, 50, 90

hanging baskets 48, 49, 50–1, 91
hedges 14, 36–7, 71
herbs 6, 12, 48, 67
hybrid berries 81

intercropping 33

jostaberries 92, 93

kale 29, 37, 54, 56–7, 89
kohlrabi 17, 35, 66, 89, 91

lamb's lettuce 57
leeks 29, 33, 35, 36, 61
lettuces 7, 12, 14, 25, 30, 33, 35, 36, 37, 46, 48, 54, 55, 85, 87, 89, 91
loganberries 81

magnesium 9
manganese 9
manure 15, 20
marjoram 48
mildew 29
minerals 9
mini vegetables 33, 66
mint 45, 67
mulches 23, 72

nectarines 71, 73, 92, 93
nitrogen 22

onion fly 28
onions 29, 35, 61, 87, 89
oregano 86, 87
Oriental vegetables 56, 87

parsley 6, 12, 33, 35, 36, 44, 48, 49, 67
parsnips 24, 29, 33, 66, 89
paths 14, 40–1
patios 18–19
peaches 71, 72, 73
pears 36, 70, 71, 92, 93
peas 17, 29, 36, 38, 63, 89
peppers 16, 17, 29, 48–9, 59, 87, 91
pests 14, 26–8, 45
planning 14–15, 19
plant plugs 25
plums 70, 71, 92, 93
pollinators 72–3
potassium 9
potagers 37, 88–9
potatoes 17, 20, 29, 47, 64, 89
potting compost 21–2
powdery mildew 29
propagators 13
pumpkins 24, 38, 39, 60

radishes 24, 33, 48, 65, 85, 87
raised beds 13, 17, 21, 34–5
raspberries 68, 74, 80, 92, 93
red spider mites 28
redcurrants 74, 75, 78–9, 92, 93
rocket 55, 89
rooftop gardens 14, 16–17, 44, 45, 90–1
root vegetables 29, 89
rootstocks, fruit trees 70–1
roquette 35
rosemary 67
rotation of crops 29
row-gardening 32–3, 36
runner beans 12, 35, 49, 62, 84, 86, 87
rusts 29

sage 6, 48, 67
salad leaves 14, 18, 55–6
savory, summer 67
seeds, sowing 19, 24–5
selenium 9
semi-circular garden 86–7
shade 13, 18
shallots 29
shelter 13, 14, 17, 18, 90
silver leaf 29
slugs 28
snails 28
soil 12–13, 15, 20–3
sowing seeds 19, 24–5
spring onions 27, 91
sprouting broccoli 29, 59, 87
squashes 38, 39, 60
step-over hedges 8, 36–7, 71
strawberries 48, 74, 76–7, 92, 93
successional planting 25
sugar snap peas 12, 35, 89, 91
summer savory 67
sunny areas 13–14, 18
supports 38–9, 47, 49, 50, 73
sweetcorn 14, 29, 63
Swiss chard 87

tayberries 92, 93
thyme 6, 48, 67, 86, 87, 92
tomatoes 17, 18, 24, 26, 29, 42, 48–9, 50, 58, 87, 90, 91
trees, fruit 72–3
turnips 29, 35, 66, 85

vine weevils 28
virus diseases 29
vitamins 9, 14

walls 12, 17, 79
watering 17, 23, 32, 47, 51, 90
weeds 32, 34, 88
whitecurrants 74, 75, 92, 93
wide rows 33
windowboxes 48, 50
winds 13, 14, 17, 72, 90
wormeries 23

zinc 9

ACKNOWLEDGEMENTS

First and foremost I would like to thank my good friend and fellow gardener Gisela Mirwis for the plans she developed for this book, as well as for her research and the notes and records she kept about the wide range of vegetables that I grow in my garden's small vegetable spaces. Thanks are also due to a number of seedsmen for their suggestions of varieties that suit small spaces. They are: Richard Massey of Marshalls (S E Marshall & Co), Colin Randel and Andrew Tokely of Thompson and Morgan, Mark Williams of Unwins, Brian Haynes of Kings Seeds, Rik Ellis of Suttons Seeds and Jeff Fothergill of Mr Fothergill's Seeds. I would like to thank Jo Belsten of the Food Research Institute, Norwich, for her comments on the nutritional value of vegetables and Sue Phillips for casting another gardener's eye over my text.

I owe thanks to a number of fellow garden writers and photographers, including Derek and Dawn St Romaine, whose urban potager is always inspirational, and Joy Larkcom for her ground-breaking books on vegetable growing. At New Holland I would like to thank Rosemary Wilkinson and Clare Johnson for their advice and encouragement; and Lisa Tai, Kate Simunek and, in particular, Gillian Haslam, for great teamwork and for putting my words into a lively and interesting shape.